HOW TO REWARD YOUR STAFF

**A Guide to Obtaining Better Performance
through the Reward System**

Martin Fisher

KOGAN
PAGE

Dedication

To June Lines, Publisher Trade Books, Kogan Page Ltd;
for all the invaluable advice and guidance she has
given to me and other authors over the years.

First published in 1995

Kogan Page Limited
120 Pentonville Road
London N1 9JN

British Library Cataloguing in Publication Data

A CIP record for this book is available from the British Library.

ISBN 0–7494–1733-1

Typeset by BookEns Ltd., Royston, Herts.
Printed and bound in Great Britain by Clays Ltd, St Ives plc.

Better Management Skills

This highly popular range of inexpensive paperbacks covers all areas of basic management. Practical, easy to read and instantly accessible, these guides will help managers to improve their business or communication skills. Those marked * are available on audio cassette.

The books in this series can be tailored to specific company requirements. For further details, please contact the publisher, Kogan Page, telephone 0171 278 0433, fax 0171 837 6348.

Be a Successful Supervisor
Business Creativity
Business Etiquette
Coaching Your Employees
Creative Decision-making
Creative Thinking in Business
Delegating for Results
Effective Employee Participation
Effective Meeting Skills
Effective Performance Appraisals*
Effective Presentation Skills
Empowerment
First Time Supervisor
Get Organised!
Goals and Goal Setting
How to Communicate Effectively*
How to Develop a Positive
    Attitude*
How to Develop Assertiveness
How to Motivate People*
How to Understand Financial
    Statements
How to Write a Staff Manual
Improving Employee
    Performance
Improving Relations at Work
Keeping Customers for Life
Leadership Skills for Women

Learning to Lead
Make Every Minute Count*
Making TQM Work
Managing Disagreement
    Constructively
Managing Organisational Change
Managing Part-time Employees
Managing Quality Customer
    Service
Managing Your Boss
Marketing for Success
Memory Skills in Business
Mentoring
Office Management
Productive Planning
Project Management
Quality Customer Service
Rate Your Skills as a Manager
Sales Training Basics
Self-managing Teams
Selling Professionally
Speed Reading in Business
Successful Negotiation
Successful Telephone Techniques
Systematic Problem-solving and
    Decision-making
Team Building
Training Methods that Work

HOW TO
REWARD
YOUR STAFF

Contents

Introduction

How to Reward Your Staff is a book for business owners, managers and those with responsibilities for personnel matters who want to know how to use rewards to get and keep the right people, and to motivate them to contribute more to the achievement of company goals.

The book will largely be about pay systems — that is, systems which achieve their objectives of attracting, retaining and motivating employees by:

- matching pay levels with market rates
- evaluating jobs to decide on their relative position in a pay structure
- developing and maintaining pay structures
- increasing motivation and rewarding achievement by paying for performance or skill
- managing the total reward system, including the provision of employee benefits
- providing managers with the scope and guidance which will enable them to manage the system effectively within their departments in order to improve motivation, commitment and performance.

The book also deals with the non-financial rewards, which can have a powerful and long-lasting effect on motivation and commitment, and do not cost anything except some effort from those who provide them.

The aim of the book is to answer a number of questions which confront all those facing the problem of managing rewards. These questions can be divided into three categories:

1. Those dealing with the foundations of all reward systems – the basic concepts and general approaches that underpin the development and operation of all such systems. These questions address the following issues:

- What can be done to improve motivation, commitment and performance through rewards?
- What are the factors which influence how people are motivated?
- What sort of rewards can managers offer which make use of these factors?
- How can these basic factors be put together into an effective reward system?

2. Those dealing with particular aspects of rewards and how they can be used effectively by managers.

- How can an organisation or a manager decide what people should be paid in relation to market rates?
- How do you establish the relative value of jobs inside the organisation?
- What sort of pay structures work best in different circumstances and how should they be designed and managed?
- How, if at all, should we differentiate pay according to performance, skill or competence?

3. Those dealing with running the reward system:

- What does the organisation do?
- What do line managers do?

How to Reward Your Staff, like other books in this series, encourages readers to learn for themselves, not only by reading, but also through questions, exercises and case studies. It can be used for individual study, workshops, seminars and formal courses.

CHAPTER 1
Improving Performance Through Rewards

How to improve organisational performance

The drive for improved organisational performance is unending. It does not matter how it is described — increasing shareholder value, achieving competitive advantage, adding value, improving the rate of return on investment, or whatever. All these add up to the same thing: doing better than your competitors by making more effective use of your resources.

As the chief executive of Boots the Chemist said recently, 'money is easy to get, good people aren't'. He also pointed out that the only thing that ultimately differentiates competitors is the quality of the people they employ.

Clearly, improving organisational performance is about improving the quality and performance of its people. But how can this be achieved? Test your own opinions by studying the following 12 propositions and deciding whether each is true or false.

IMPROVING PERFORMANCE

	True	False
1. Improving the performance of people is simply a matter of exercising strong direction and control.	____	____
2. Improving performance is largely a matter of better selection and training.	____	____
3. People only work harder if you offer them more money.	____	____
4. Pay is a key factor in attracting and retaining high quality people.	____	____
5. Incentive schemes may increase output but they can adversely affect quality.	____	____
6. Pay-for-performance schemes can be better at demotivating than motivating people.	____	____
7. People will be motivated to work harder and better by rewards, but only if they feel they are worthwhile and believe they have a good chance of obtaining them.	____	____
8. The motivational impact of a pay increase quickly disappears.	____	____
9. Pay will only work well as a motivator if it is felt to be fair.	____	____
10. Non-financial rewards such as praise, recognition and the opportunity to achieve and develop can have a deeper and longer lasting positive effect on motivation than financial rewards.	____	____
11. People work best if they are committed to agreed objectives.	____	____
12. Valuing employees is a matter of using both financial and non-financial rewards.	____	____

Comments on these propositions follow.

Improving the performance of people is simply a matter of exercising strong direction and control

This is the leadership theory of motivation. Strong leaders get results — which, of course, is true up to a point. Strong leaders can sometimes be good at making plans for other people to carry out and equally good at taking the credit if things go well and blaming the people at the sharp end if things go wrong. Some politicians fall into this category.

Strong direction and control *can* get results but obedience and fear of being found out is only one way of motivation, and it is by no means the best one.

Improving performance is largely a matter of better selection and training

Selecting the right people and providing them with relevant and performance-related training is clearly an important factor in improving performance. And effective leaders are good at both these things. But it is not the only route. You may have experienced and qualified people in the job, but how can you guarantee that they will produce the results you want? Motivation *and* ability need to come into the equation. In fact, you can say: Performance = Motivation × Ability; you need both (note that the performance equation is not Motivation + Ability, which would indicate, erroneously, that one or the other would suffice on its own).

People only work harder if you offer them more money

This proposition is at the heart of many approaches to pay. In effect, many reward systems are based on the belief that people only work for money and therefore money is the only way to get them to work. Of course, money is important to everyone, except hermits, if only to ensure survival. But the degree to which it is important varies. It is a truism — common sense — to say that everybody is different. But the truth of truisms is not always self-evident and common sense is not all that common.

Pay is a key factor in attracting and retaining high quality people

What attracts people to move to a new job? For some it will be the opportunity to take a career step – to gain wider and higher-level experience and to have greater responsibilities. Others will seek security or, if they are out of a job, any port in a storm. But to most people the pay will be an all-important consideration. They will have cast their eye over the job market and assessed what they are worth. If they are being paid below what they think their market rate is, they are likely to want to make a move. So pay is a very important factor in attracting people.

Pay is equally important in retaining them, for the same reason. People generally have a pretty good idea of what they are worth in the market-place and, if the opportunity arises, they will want to realise their worth. They may also be concerned about career prospects and security, but pay will be a major consideration. This is why one of the main criteria for a good pay system is that it should be externally competitive, which means that if a company wants to attract and retain good quality employees it must constantly track market rates and do its best to match or even surpass them.

Incentive schemes may increase output but they can adversely affect quality

One of the main purposes of incentive schemes is to get people to work harder. And they can succeed in doing this if:

- the reward is clearly linked to the effort
- individuals can control their pace of work
- the reward is worth having
- the pay-off takes place quickly.

The sorts of job which are most likely to satisfy these criteria include those in which employees are engaged in unit or small batch production (eg garment making, hand fabrication of parts), selling, and any job in which the worker directly controls the units produced.

The problem is that if you ask people to concentrate on output and pay them accordingly, they will tend to go for volume and pay little regard to quality. Shoddy work and a high percentage of rejects may occur in a manufacturing environment, and sales representatives will concentrate on those products which are easiest to sell rather than those generating the highest margin. Quantity is achieved at the expense of quality.

It is because of these problems that many quality-conscious companies have abandoned piece work for a high day rate (ie a high basic rate) which is topped up by bonuses which may be related as much to quality as to quantity.

Pay-for-performance schemes can be better at demotivating than motivating people

People will only be motivated by a pay-for-performance scheme if they feel that they are being fairly rewarded in relation to the effort or contribution they make. Many schemes, especially performance-related pay (PRP) systems, signally fail to convince staff that they are fair. One good example is the PRP scheme originally introduced by the Inland Revenue (who ought to know about money, if anyone does). Research into how the scheme was working conducted by Marsden and Richardson of the London School of Economics established that the scheme was generally felt to be completely unfair by managers and other employees alike, and it was remarkably successful as a means of demotivating people – hardly the intention. It has now been replaced.

It is a well-established fact that getting PRP, or indeed any variety of pay-for-performance scheme, right, is one of the most difficult tasks any management can undertake. They often get it wrong. PRP is not a panacea to be introduced lightly.

People will only be motivated by worthwhile rewards which they expect to get

The truth of this proposition appears to be self-evident. But is it astonishing how many organisations introduce pay-for-performance schemes with high hopes but with minuscule returns.

Just as bad, if not worse, are the schemes where expectations of a reward are minimised because there is an obscure or even completely hidden relationship between what people do and what they get.

The motivational impact of a pay increase quickly disappears

Research has shown that an increase in pay, even a substantial one, may cause satisfaction at the time but this feeling seldom lasts long. The increase is quickly absorbed into a readjusted budget and is soon taken for granted. It has been said that 'people are wanting animals' and this certainly seems to apply to matters of pay. However much they get, a lot of people want more. Even in the short term the motivational effect of a pay increase which is an 'across-the-board' one following a negotiation or a cost-of-living award is likely to be negligible. And this is also the case with the almost automatic increases which come annually to those on incremental scales.

Pay will only work as a motivator if it is felt to be fair

The 'felt fair' principle states that people will only be motivated by their pay if they believe it is fair in relation to their contribution and effort and, importantly, in relation to what other people are paid within the organisation. Internal equity – a fair system for determining pay levels and rewards – is therefore an important consideration to those responsible for designing and maintaining reward policies. Job evaluation schemes as described in Chapter 6, and pay structures, which are covered in Chapter 7, need to demonstrate that the system is fair.

The long-lasting impact of non-financial rewards

Non-financial rewards focus on the needs most people have, although to different degrees, for achievement, recognition, responsibility, influence and personal growth. These needs are related to the content of the job or what is sometimes called 'the quality of working life'. Their satisfaction can be described as a process of intrinsic motivation, or motivation by the work itself. Intrinsic motivation can have a longer-term and deeper effect than the extrinsic motivation provided by financial incentives because, by definition, the intrinsic motivators are inherent in individuals and are not imposed from outside, although they may be encouraged by the organisation.

Commitment to objectives

Douglas McGregor's 'theory Y' states that: 'Commitment to objectives is a function of the rewards associated with their achievement'.

This suggests a very important principle which underpins all effective reward systems: people will be most highly motivated when they are clear about what they are expected to achieve and know that they will be rewarded appropriately if they do achieve their agreed objectives.

Valuing employees

Everyone wants to be valued – for themselves and for their achievements. Hence the importance of the non-financial rewards – the intrinsic motivators – which aim to give people the opportunity to do valuable work and to be appreciated for it. But it is also necessary to put money where your mouth is. Praise is a powerful motivator but the tangible recognition of achievement by a financial award can be even more powerful. You need both. It is interesting to note that the award of an achievement bonus in the form of a reasonably substantial lump-sum payment which can be spent on something worthwhile *now*, can make more impact than an increase in salary where the reward is spread over a year and can easily be absorbed into normal month-by-month expenditure.

So what do you think of these comments on the 12 propositions you considered earlier?
Tick one only:

1. ☐ I agree that improving performance through rewards is a highly complex process which takes a lot of effort to get right.

2. ☐ I am still convinced that improving performance is about money. People want money and they will work harder and perform better to get more of it.

If you ticked the first comment then you recognise that there are no simplistic answers to improving performance through rewards. If you and your organisation want to get the best results from people it is necessary to:

- understand what makes people tick — ie the process of motivation — and how rewards can best motivate them
- appreciate the value of the different types of reward and how they can best be used
- consider in the light of this understanding what sort of reward system is going to work best for you in your particular circumstances; this means developing a system which is externally competitive as well as being internally equitable and which rewards people properly according to their levels of competence and contribution.

These issues are addressed in the next three chapters and amplified later.

If you ticked the second comment you are in very good company — this is what many managers believe. And, of course, they are right. Money is a powerful motivator because, as will be discussed in the next chapter, it is a means of satisfying most of our needs, although possibly on a short-term basis. However, you still have to work hard to get the money right. The financial reward system will not work if:

- market rates are not tracked carefully
- it is patently unfair because there is no logical, objective or consistent basis for deciding what people should be paid
- the pay structure is incoherent and does not provide for people to be rewarded according to the level of their contribution

● pay-for-performance schemes are badly conceived and poorly executed, as they often are.

These specific issues are all considered in Chapters 5 to 8, but they need to be addressed in the light of an understanding of the basic principles of reward management, as discussed in Chapters 2 to 4.

The last two chapters of this book bring everything together by considering, overall, what the organisation and individual managers need to do to improve performance through the reward system.

CHAPTER 2
Motivating Through Rewards

What is motivation about?

Highly motivated people make things happen. They know what they want or need to do and then they do it, successfully. They proceed purposefully towards the achievement of their own goals and those of the organisation.

To motivate people is to ensure that they move in the direction you want them to go. This may not, of course, be where *they* want to go. Everyone has their own set of needs and wants and the aim of motivation is to bring those in line with the organisation's requirements and your own needs as a manager. Some people put it very crudely, saying in effect: 'you must get them to do what you want them to do, whether they want to do it or not'. Adopting this attitude will not get you very far. You may or may not obtain grudging submission; you certainly will not get willing cooperation.

Ideally, you should aim to integrate the needs of individuals with the needs of the organisation and your needs as a manager in the organisation. The principle of integration means that in satisfying their own needs employees will also satisfy the needs of the organisation, and this principle underpins most satisfactory approaches to reward management.

To put this principle into practice, however, it is a good idea to have some understanding of motivation theory – what makes people tick. And remember, if you recoil from the word theory, that there is nothing so practical as a *good* theory – one which is based on down-to-earth research on what actually happens, on experimentation, and on analysis of experience. Such a theory will have been put to the test in real life in offices, laboratories, out in the field and on the shop floor, and it is certainly better than the assumptions based on folk-lore or myths which many people make when considering motivation. A considerable proportion of this chapter is therefore devoted to exploring the practical realities of motivation theory as applied to managing rewards.

The process of motivation

The process of motivation is initiated by someone recognising an unsatisfied need. A goal is then established which, it is thought, will satisfy the need, and a course of action is determined which is expected to lead towards the attainment of the goal and the satisfaction of the need. This process is illustrated as a continuous cycle in Figure 2.1. The cycle is continuous because as one need is satisfied another surfaces – we tend not to be satisfied with what we get, we generally want more.

People are motivated by rewards and incentives which will enable them to satisfy their needs or will provide them with goals to attain – as long as those goals are worthwhile *and* attainable. But the needs of individuals and the goals

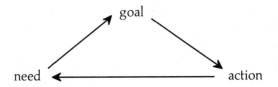

Figure 2.1 *The process of motivation*

associated with them vary so widely that it is difficult, if not impossible, to predict with any precision how a particular award or incentive will affect individual behaviour.

Types of motivation

Motivation at work can take place in two ways:

1. *Intrinsic motivation.* This is derived from the content of the job. It is motivation by the work itself in that what people do satisfies their need for achievement, recognition, responsibility and personal growth.
2. *Extrinsic motivation.* This is what is done to and for people to motivate them. It arises when management provides such awards as increased pay, praise or promotion. When the motivating impact of pay-for-performance schemes is discussed this is the type of motivation to which people are referring.

Extrinsic motivators can have an immediate effect on performance, but this will not necessarily last. The intrinsic motivators, which are concerned with the quality of working life, are likely to have a deeper and longer-term effect because they are inherent in people and not imposed from outside, although they may be nurtured by the organisation.

Basic concepts of motivation

The basic concepts of motivation are concerned with needs, goals, reinforcement, expectations and equity.

Needs
Needs theory states that behaviour is motivated by unsatisfied needs. The key needs associated with work are those for achievement, recognition, responsibility, influence and personal growth.

Goals

Goals theory suggests that motivation can be increased by goal-setting processes with the following characteristics:

- goals are specific
- goals are challenging but realisable
- they are seen as fair and reasonable
- individuals participate fully in goal-setting
- feedback ensures that people get a feeling of pride and satisfaction from the experience of achieving a challenging but fair goal
- feedback is used to gain commitment to even higher goals.

Reinforcement

Reinforcement indicates that successes in achieving goals and rewards act as positive incentives and reinforce the successful behaviour, which is repeated the next time a similar need arises.

Expectations (expectancy theory)

This states that motivation takes place when individuals:

- feel able to change their behaviour
- feel confident that a change in their behaviour will produce a reward
- value the reward sufficiently to justify the change in behaviour.

Expectancy theory boils down to two common sense propositions:

- if people don't know what they're going to get, they won't want to get it
- even if people *do* know what they're going to get, but it is not worth getting, they still won't want to get it.

It is astonishing how often these eminently sensible points have been totally ignored by those who advocate or design performance-related pay schemes.

Equity

To be equitable and therefore to motivate, or at least not to demotivate, pay must be felt to match the level of work and the capacity of the individual. In other words, to be effective, a reward system must be felt to be fair. This is often called the 'felt-fair' principle.

Implications

The following are some of the typical beliefs people have about motivation. In the light of motivation theory as outlined above and your own experiences, rate the extent to which you agree or disagree with them on a scale of 5 to 1 (5 = fully agree, 1 = completely disagree).

1. Individual needs are almost infinitely variable.
2. To motivate people it is necessary to use both intrinsic and extrinsic motivating factors, but it is impossible to generalise on what the best mix of these is likely to be.
3. Money is a key motivating factor.
4. To motivate people it is simply necessary to spell out to them what they have to do and what will happen if they don't do it.
5. Motivation is a matter of setting and agreeing demanding but achievable goals.
6. Pay may well be the best motivator but it is only fully effective if the reward people expect to get is worthwhile and they feel they can achieve it.
7. Praise (recognition of achievement) is one of the most powerful motivators.
8. Irrespective of the size of their rewards, people will be demotivated if they feel that the pay system is unfair.

Comments on these beliefs

1. Individual needs *do* vary considerably although they can often focus on one thing, eg more money. But it is dangerous to generalise that any one approach to motivation is likely to work equally well for everybody.

For some people, long-term security or job satisfaction may be more important than financial rewards.

2. To recognise the variety of individual needs it is best to offer a mix of motivators. Pay is obviously important but it needs to be reinforced by other non-financial motivators such as praise and recognition. For many people, the strongest and longest-lasting type of motivation will be the intrinsic motivators – opportunities to achieve, to exercise responsibility and to advance their careers.

3. Money is of course the key motivator for many people but unless the pay system is fair and carefully managed, it can be a demotivating factor. In any case, its impact will be considerably reinforced if other non-financial motivators are used.

4. It is clearly necessary for people to know what they are expected to do but they will be more motivated if they have contributed to the agreement of their goals rather than having them 'spelt out'. To rely on threats as a means of motivation is clearly not likely to get you very far.

5. Goal setting is a key part of the motivation process. But goals have to be demanding *and* achievable and they will work best if they have been agreed.

6. Too many performance-pay schemes offer rewards which are hardly worth having and/or are perceived as being unattainable. These are the approaches which have brought many performance-related pay (PRP) schemes into disrepute.

7. Praise is a highly appreciated reward and can be an effective motivator. But it must be deserved and given sincerely.

Relative importance of motivators

Mark the following motivators on a scale of 1 (little importance) to 10 (highly important):

- The incentive/reward system ....
- Leadership by managers ....
- Influence of work colleagues ....
- Strength of needs and wants. ....

You may well have given the incentive/reward system top marks, but the effectiveness of this as a motivator depends largely on the capabilities of those who run the system. Rewards don't work by themselves; they have to be managed carefully. Neither can you ignore the influence of colleagues who can spur people on or hold them back. Creating a situation where teams work effectively together in agreeing and achieving goals can be a good way of improving individual motivation.

Finally, it has to be recognised that some people will be self-motivated – they set themselves targets and then go for them – while with others, the motivational drive will be much lower. People in the former category may not need to be motivated by management but they should still be rewarded appropriately in line with their contribution or they will rapidly become demotivated and go to a company where their talents will be properly recognised. Those in the latter category *will* need encouragement with incentives and rewards which are focused on their particular needs.

Focusing on the key motivators
Complete the following statements in the light of the circumstances in your company or department:

1. The key motivators are:

   ● for directors_____
   ● for managers _____
   ● for professional/technical staff _____
   ● for office staff_____
   ● for skilled workers_____
   ● for semi-skilled workers _____

2. My reasons in each case for believing that these are the key motivators are:

   ● director_____
   ● managers_____

- professional/technical staff _____
- office staff _____
- skilled workers_____
- semi-skilled/unskilled workers _____

3. To get the best out of these motivators we should:

  _____

  _____

  _____

CHAPTER 3
The Choice of Rewards

Many people concentrate on the direct motivation which they hope will be provided by incentives and bonuses, without giving enough consideration to base pay and other forms of financial reward or benefit. Even more people neglect the importance of non-financial rewards as motivators. But these are all part of the total reward system and this chapter examines in turn each of the following types of reward which will be catered for in a comprehensive system:

- Financial rewards
- Non-financial rewards
- Employee benefits
- Rewards in kind.

Financial rewards

Financial rewards consist of the base pay, differential payments, ie extra pay (incentives and bonuses) for performance, skill or competence, and payments for special working arrangements and conditions or additional responsibility.

Base pay
Base pay is the rate for the job, without any additional

payments. On the shop floor it can be called day rate, time rate or base rate. The base rate is fixed by reference to market rates, what other employees in the company are paid, the grade allocated to the job in a job-evaluated pay structure or by negotiation with trade unions nationally, locally or within the company. The basic pay may be related to market rates in accordance with the policy of the company. This pay policy may be to:

- *Pay above market rates.* This policy is sometimes expressed as 'we aim to pay at the upper quartile of market rates'. The upper quartile is the point in a range of numbers above which one-quarter of the individual numbers fall. Thus if a range of numbers (a distribution) were 3, 5, 7, 9, 11, 13, 15, 17, 19 the upper quartile figure would be 15. Data on market rates often records the dispersion of the individual rate collected in a market rate survey in terms of upper and lower quartiles and the median (see below). If all companies actually paid above market rates a permanent inflationary situation would result. Fortunately, they do not and many which aspire to pay 'upper quartile' rates fail to do so.
- *Match market rates*, ie pay average or 'median' rates. A median is the mid-point in a range of numbers.
- *Pay below market rate*, eg at the lower quartile (the number in the range below which one-quarter of the individual numbers fall − 7 in the above example).

Performance pay
Performance-related pay or incentive schemes provide for the differential payment to be directly related to performance as assessed in an appraisal scheme, to output or to some other measure such as sales, added value, profitability, or increase in shareholder value. Incentives provided in a performance-related pay scheme may be paid as a permanent increase to the base rate. In a shop floor incentive scheme, payouts will be made periodically as additions to the basic rate for the job.

Incentives are forward looking. They are designed to

motivate people to achieve higher levels of performance. Rewards are retrospective payments which recognise achievements but can also act as an incentive in the sense of encouraging people to continue performing well in the hope of a future reward.

Incentives should be distinguished from bonuses. Incentives are payments linked to the achievement of previously set and agreed objectives and targets. They aim to motivate people to achieve higher levels of performance by means of rewards which are in fixed proportion to the extent to which a target has been achieved.

Bonuses

Bonuses are rewards for success. They are paid out in lump sums and include various forms of executive bonus schemes and 'achievement' bonuses. Many companies are now using the latter as the major form of reward above basic pay on the grounds that, as long as the base rate is competitive, the most effective form of financial reward is a bonus which is focused on a particular achievement, or which can be related to a sustained period of high-level performance. It can be argued that a lump-sum of 5 per cent of pay would make a more powerful impact than a 5 per cent increase in basic rate. The former can be spent on something really needed now, while the latter will be absorbed into the monthly expenditure budget and taken for granted.

From the company's point of view it can also be argued that a permanent pay-for-performance increase to a salary is in effect an annuity. It may have been earned that year, but will it go on being earned? Regular increments can result in employees being seriously overpaid in relation to what they do and contribute. A bonus can be related to current performance and has to be re-earned next year.

Bonuses can be paid out to individuals or to teams. There is now increasing emphasis on team pay to recognise the growing importance of teamwork in organisations.

Company-wide bonuses paid out through profit sharing or gain sharing can provide general rewards which are related to company profits or added value. They may not provide a direct individual incentive but they can increase commitment and identification with the business.

Skill/competence-based pay
Pay may be linked to the skill or competence level achieved by individuals as long as the skills or competences are relevant to the job. (Competences describe the capacity of individuals to do jobs and the behaviour expected of them if they are to perform a task satisfactorily.) Skill/competence-based pay is being used by some companies with highly skilled or well-qualified employees who work flexibly and whose contribution depends entirely on the level of skill or competence they possess. Such companies believe that skill/competence-based pay is a better way of rewarding people than incentive schemes based on artificial and often unmeasurable targets. Skill/competence-based pay may be linked to the achievement of NVQs (National Vocational Qualifications).

Special payments
Special payments include those made for working overtime shifts, unsocial hours, or for unpleasant or dangerous conditions. They may also comprise 'responsibility allowances' for carrying out tasks which are not normally part of the job.

Non-financial rewards

Non-financial rewards are related to the needs people have for achievement, recognition, responsibility, influence and personal growth. The degree to which these needs are powerful motivators will vary between different people and to be effective they have to be used selectively on an individual basis.

Achievement
Achievement can be defined as the need for success measured against a personal standard of excellence. An American

researcher, David McClelland, studied a number of successful managers and established that their major needs and, therefore, motivators, were achievement, power and 'affiliation', ie wanting to be on good terms with other people. Of these three, achievement was the strongest motivator in the most successful managers.

What is sometimes called 'achievement motivation' can be increased by organisations through processes such as:

- *Job design* – structuring jobs to give people the maximum scope to use their abilities.
- *Empowerment* – giving people more control over, and responsibility for, their work, and ensuring that they have the knowledge and skills to do it to the satisfaction of both the organisation and themselves.
- *Performance management* – a process of managing performance which uses an agreed framework of objectives, standards and performance improvement and development plans and relies on feedback and reinforcement as a means of motivating people.
- *Skill/competence-based pay* – rewarding people according to the level of skill or competence they achieve.

Recognition

Recognition is one of the most effective means of rewarding, and therefore motivating, people. People need to know not only how well they have achieved their objectives or carried out their work but also that their achievements are appreciated and that they are valued accordingly.

Recognition can, of course, be achieved by financial means. An achievement bonus is a highly tangible way of showing appreciation. However, you cannot always be handing out bonuses, but you can give recognition as and when it is deserved by providing positive feedback (informing people that you have noticed their achievement) and praise (commending them on what they have done).

Praise, however, should be given judiciously. It should be related to real achievements. Praise which is insincere because managers are going through the motions can have a negative effect.

Recognition can also be provided by managers who listen to and act upon the suggestions of their team members and, importantly, acknowledge their contribution.

Actions which can also provide recognition include promotion, allocation to a high-profile project, enlargement of the job to provide scope for more interesting and rewarding work, and various forms of status symbols. For example, nominating a 'sales representative of the month' and publishing it throughout the sales force is a valuable way of providing public recognition. Other ways of recognising people include:

- A well-publicised trip to, say, the company's headquarters in the United States
- The use of a superior car
- An article in the company magazine
- A news item on notice boards
- A special badge.

Responsibility
People can be motivated by being given more responsibility for their own work. This is what empowerment is about and is in line with the concept of intrinsic motivation related to the content of the job mentioned in the last chapter.

For jobs to be intrinsically motivating, individuals:

- must receive meaningful feedback about their performance
- must feel that they are able to use their abilities to perform the job well
- should have a high degree of self-control over setting their own goals and over defining the paths that they should follow to achieve these goals.

This approach to motivating through responsibility follows Douglas McGregor's *Theory Y:* 'The average human being learns, under proper conditions, not only to accept but also to seek responsibility'.

Of course, if you enlarge or enrich jobs to increase responsibility, people may want more pay, but if they deserve it, why not? You would then be combining financial and non-financial means of motivation to good effect.

Influence
People can be motivated by the drive to exert influence or to exercise power, the latter being one of the prime motivators for many people with ambition. Through its policies for employee involvement, a business can provide for motivation and increased commitment by encouraging people to express their views and by listening to and acting on those views. This is another aspect of empowerment.

Personal growth
Increasingly, people at all levels in organisations recognise the importance of continually upgrading their skills and of pro-gressively developing their careers. This is the philosophy of continuous development. Many employees regard access to training as a key element in the overall reward package. The availability of learning opportunities, the selection of individuals for high-prestige training programmes and the emphasis placed by the company on learning new skills as well as improving existing ones, can all act as strong motivating forces.

Employee benefits

Employee benefits are elements of the total reward package which provide extra value for employees beyond their pay. Benefits include items to which a financial value can be attached, such as pension schemes, insurance, sick pay and company cars. They also include terms of employment such as holidays which are not strictly remuneration.

Employee benefits are sometimes referred to derogatively as 'fringe benefits', but they are, in fact, essential elements in the reward package which, even though they will not provide direct motivation, can increase commitment and a general feeling of satisfaction with the company.

Rewards in kind

Rewards in kind — gifts, holidays, 'candle-lit dinners for two', are often handed out to sales representatives for success in a sales competition, or for achieving an exceptional result. Increasingly, companies are offering rewards in kind to other staff. A weekend in Paris for two can often make more of an impact than a bonus or a lump-sum payment which may too easily be dissipated on mundane expenditures. Rewards in kind are, however, taxable.

The total reward package

Tick one only:

1. ☐ I recognise that to get the best out of people I have to think in terms of a total reward package which contains a mix of approaches to motivation and gaining commitment.
2. ☐ I still think it is best to concentrate on the immediate and tangible forms of reward provided by incentives and bonuses which will provide direct motivation.

Elements of the total reward package
If you have ticked (1), think about your own company or department (or another organisation you know about) and complete the following statements in a way which would be most appropriate to the particular circumstances (ie the type of company or department, the product or process, the type of people employed, and the 'corporate culture' — the 'way things are done around here'; what is believed to be important and how people normally behave.

1. In our (my) circumstances, I feel we ought to pay more attention to:

- Financial rewards.
- Non-financial rewards.
- Employee benefits.

- Rewards in kind.
- An appropriate mix of the above.

2. The best form of financial rewards would be:

_____

3. I believe the following non-financial rewards would be
   most significant:

_____

4. This is how I would want to develop the financial rewards
   part of the package:

_____

5. This is how I feel the best use could be made of the non-
   financial rewards: _____

_____

If you have ticked (2) remember that, however strong a case
there is for focusing on direct benefits, you still have to work
very hard to get the system right. And this is what will be
discussed in the rest of this book.

CHAPTER 4
The Total Reward System

The total reward system, as described in Chapter 3, comprises the core elements of base pay and certain benefits such as holidays, sick pay and, usually, pensions. In addition, and importantly, the system incorporates the various forms of non-financial rewards which satisfy individual needs for recognition, responsibility, achievement and personal growth. The reward system may also contain elements of differential pay (payments for performance, skill or competence) and extra 'fringe' benefits such as company cars or medical insurance. The total reward system should be underpinned by defined objectives, strategies and policies as described in this chapter.

Objectives of a reward system

The objectives of a reward system can be to:

- *Compete in the job market* – attract and retain high quality people.
- *Motivate members of the organisation* – achieve superior levels of quality performance.
- *Encourage value-added performance* – achieve continuous improvement by focusing attention on areas where the maximum added value can be obtained from improved performance and by getting people to agree to demanding goals in those areas which match their capability.

- *Increase commitment* – ensure that members of the organisation develop a strong belief in the organisation and identify with its mission, strategies and values.
- *Achieve fairness and equity* – reward people fairly and consistently according to their contribution.
- *Support culture change* – provide levers for changing the organisation's culture as expressed by its values and norms for performance, innovation, risk-taking, quality, flexibility and teamworking.
- *Achieve integration* – function as an integral part of the management processes of the organisation. Reward management should be a key component in a mutually reinforcing and coherent range of human resource management processes.
- *Support managers* – provide them with the authority and skills needed to use rewards to help them achieve their goals. It is necessary, however, to ensure that managers have a strong framework of guiding principles and procedures, within which they can play their part in managing rewards for their staff with whatever guidance they may need.
- *Empower individuals and teams* – use the total reward system to raise performance and quality through empowered people who have the scope and skills needed to succeed and are rewarded accordingly. Reward processes should help to upgrade competence and encourage personal development.
- *Support new developments* – help in the introduction and effective use of sophisticated management techniques, for example, JIT (just-in-time), FMS (flexible manufacturing systems), cellular manufacturing, CIM (computer-integrated manufacturing) and other applications of information technology such as integrated business systems and point-of-event data capture systems.
- *Enhance quality* – help to achieve continuous improvement in levels of quality and customer service by supporting such processes as TQM (total quality management).
- *Promote teamworking* – assist in improving cooperation and effective teamworking at all levels.

- *Encourage flexibility* – help to achieve the most efficient use of human resources through job-based, skills-based, and organisation-based flexibility arrangements.
- *Provide value for money* – assess the costs as well as the benefits of reward management practices and ensure that they are operated cost-effectively.

Reward strategies

Reward strategies should be founded on the proposition that the ultimate source of value is people. This means that reward processes must respond creatively to their needs as well as to those of the organisation. The basis of the strategies will be the organisation's requirements for performance in the short and longer term as expressed in its corporate strategies. Reward strategies should be business driven, responding to the needs of the business to compete, grow and innovate, but they also provide levers for change, reinforcing and validating the thrust of the business.

The reward strategy will mainly be concerned with the direction the organisation should follow in developing the right mix and levels of financial and non-financial rewards in order to support the business strategy. The reward strategy will be concerned with:

- the demands of the business strategy, including cost constraints;
- meeting objectives for the attraction and retention of high quality employees;
- how superior performance and performance improvement can be motivated and reinforced;
- the development of pay structures which are competitive in the market-place and are performance-driven;
- ensuring that reward policies are used to convey messages about the expectations and values of the organisation;
- achieving the right balance between rewards for individual, team and organisational performance;
- evolving total reward processes which incorporate the best

mix of financial and non-financial rewards and employee benefits;
- achieving the flexibility required when administering reward processes within fast-changing organisations existing in highly competitive or turbulent environments;
- fitting reward processes to the individual needs and expectations of employees.

The reward strategy should be backed up by a realistic action plan and should incorporate an assessment of risks and contingency plans if things go wrong. Arrangements should also be made to ensure that the results of implementing a reward strategy are evaluated against its objectives and cost budgets.

Reward policies

Reward strategies indicate broadly where you are going; reward policies tell you how you are going to get there. Express your understanding of reward policies in your organisation by ticking the appropriate boxes below.

Level of rewards
Tick one only:

1. ☐ Our policy is to pay above the market rate.
2. ☐ Our policy is to match the market rate, as far as possible.

Market rate and equity
Tick one only:

1. ☐ Our rates of pay are market driven – we pay whatever is necessary in the market-place to get and keep the people we need even if it upsets internal differentials.
2. ☐ We believe that our first priority is to preserve internal equity; to pay people according to their relative contribution within the organisation. Only in very

exceptional circumstances would we pay more to match market rates.

Differential rewards
Tick one only:

1. ☐ We believe that reward should be differentiated according to performance. This is because we see it as a major method of motivating people as well as a clear indication that we mean business when we press for performance improvements.
2. ☐ We are against paying for performance because we do not believe that any performance pay scheme can operate fairly or provide value for money.

Flexibility
Tick one only:

1. ☐ We believe that our priority is to adopt pay policies which are applied consistently throughout the organisation.
2. ☐ We acknowledge that a flexible approach to pay is necessary to reflect different individual and organisational needs.

Employee involvement
Tick one only:

1. ☐ Reward policies and practices are the concern of management – employees need not be involved.
2. ☐ It is essential to involve employees in developing aspects of reward practices, such as job evaluation, to convince them that the system is fair.

Communicating to employees
Tick one only:

1. ☐ It is essential to keep our staff fully informed of our

pay policies and practices and how they will benefit from them.

2. ☐ Special efforts are not needed to communicate our pay policies to staff.

Affordability
Tick one only:

1. ☐ Our pay practices must be entirely governed by our ability to afford the costs involved.
2. ☐ We may sometimes have to recognise that the development of competitive pay practices is an investment we cannot afford not to make.

Comments
The issues involved in developing reward policies are considered below.

Level of reward
The policy on the level of reward indicates whether the company is a high payer, is content to pay median or average rates of pay or even, exceptionally, accepts that it has to pay below the average. Pay policy, which is sometimes referred to as the 'pay stance' or 'pay posture' of a company, will depend on a number of factors. These include the extent to which the company demands high levels of performance from its employees, the degree to which there is competition for good quality people, the traditional stance of the company, the organisation culture, and whether or not it can or should afford to be a high payer.

Policies on pay levels will also refer to differentials and the number of steps or grades that should exist in the pay hierarchy. This will be influenced by the structure of the company. In today's flatter organisations, an extended or complex pay hierarchy may not be required on the grounds that it will constrain the flexible movement of people in the organisation.

Market rate and equity

A policy needs to be formulated on the extent to which rewards are market driven (externally competitive) rather than internally equitable (paying people according to the relative value of their jobs within the organisation). Any company which has to attract and retain staff who are much in demand and where market rates are therefore high, may, to a degree, have to sacrifice the ideals of equity to the realism of the market-place. The pay management process must cope as best it can when the irresistible force of the market-place meets the immovable object of internal equity. There will also be some degree of tension in these circumstances, and while no solution will ever be simple or entirely satisfactory, there is one basic principle which can enhance the likelihood of success. That principle is to make explicit and fully identifiable the compromises with internal equity that are made in response to market pressures.

Differential pay

Pay policy will need to determine whether or not the organisation wants to pay for performance, skill or competence and if so, how much and under what circumstances. There may, for example, be a policy that bonuses should be paid for exceptional performance but that to be significant, they should not be less than, say, 10 per cent of basic pay, while their upper limit should be restricted to 30 per cent or so of basic pay. The policy may also indicate the approach to be used in relating pay to individual, team or organisational performance. Some organisations are against performance pay in principle because they feel that it is difficult to operate fairly or to achieve the improvements in performance it is expected to provide. Increasingly, organisations are turning towards some form of payment for additional skills or competences as long as they contribute to high levels of performance.

Flexibility

Reward policies have to take into account the extent to which reward processes should operate flexibly in response to fast-changing conditions, the adoption of less rigid organisation structures and approaches to management, and changes or variations in the needs of the company or its employees.

Involving employees

Pay policies and practices are more likely to be accepted and understood and, therefore, be more effective if employees are involved in their design and management. This particularly applies to job evaluation and methods of measuring and assessing performance, and relating rewards to that performance (performance management and paying for performance processes).

Communicating to employees

Pay processes are powerful media for conveying messages to employees about the organisation's values and the contribution staff are expected to make to upholding those values and achieving the organisation's goals. They should not, however, be left to speak for themselves. It is essential to communicate to individuals, teams and representative bodies what the processes are setting out to do, how it is proposed to do it, how they affect them, how recipients will benefit, and the part individuals and teams will be expected to play. It is particularly important to explain the basis of any pay-for-performance scheme and also to convey to employees how their total remuneration package of pay and other benefits is made up.

Affordability

Ultimately, all pay policies have to relate to what the business can afford to pay, although there may be circumstances when it is necessary to take a long-term view and pay highly to attract or retain good quality staff, even when in the short term the company cannot really afford the cost.

Fitting pay policies and practices to the business

Pay policies and practices must generally fit the particular circumstances, culture and management style of the business. But there are circumstances where they can be used as levers for change, focusing attention on key performance issues.

Here are some miniature case studies. Set out beneath each case the general line you think the organisation should take in developing its pay policies and practices.

Case study 1
The organisation is a large and well-established insurance company. At present, the procedure for handling underwriting proposals and claims is on a production line basis, which involves individuals dealing with one small part of the process and then passing it down the line for the next part to be performed. It has, however, been decided to handle these matters on a team basis. The members of each team will be responsible for dealing with all the underwriting and claims processing, sharing the responsibility for delivering the required results and operating on a flexible 'multiskilled' basis, ie each fully competent member is expected to be able to undertake any task which has to be carried out by the team. At present there is an individual merit pay scheme which is based on ratings made by managers.

Case study 2
The company is an electronics manufacturing organisation which is about to open on a green-field site in South Wales. Staff will be specially trained to carry out assembly work on a production line. A JIT (just-in-time) system will be operated.

Case study 3
This is a bio-chemical business which carries out research and development of entirely new products. It is a high-tech environment and a high proportion of staff are qualified scientists.

Case study 4
The company is an old, established manufacturing concern which is stagnating. Productivity and quality levels are not matching their competitors'. A new chief executive wants to develop a more performance- and quality-oriented culture.

Comments on case studies
1. To get teams working effectively together the best approach would be to abandon the existing individual merit rating scheme and replace it with a team pay system. This would provide for team members to share a bonus, which would be based on the extent to which team targets have been achieved. The pay of individuals should be related to the degree to which their level of competence enables them to play a full and flexible role as members of a team.

2. In this case the requirement is for employees to keep pace with the production line to ensure that the JIT system works. But they must also be 'right first time', ie they have to meet stringent quality standards. This is a high day-rate environment − it is not appropriate for any form of individual incentive scheme. Group bonuses could, however, be shared out on the basis of production line performance on such aspects as productivity, inventory levels, delivery-on-time and quality (number of rejects or errors).

3. This is a situation in which scientists are engaged in innovatory project work over long time-scales. It is not possible, therefore, to provide differential pay which is related to short-term results. The company depends entirely on the skills and expertise of these scientists and their pay should therefore be related to the level of competence they have achieved.

4. In this company pay arrangements can provide leverage for cultural change. A performance-related pay scheme can be introduced to deliver the message that high levels of performance will be rewarded appropriately.

CHAPTER 5
Finding Out Market Rates

You need to know about market rates — what other organisations pay for similar jobs — for the following reasons:

- to gain information on external relativities;
- to attract good candidates to respond to your job advertisements;
- to retain good quality employees who might otherwise leave for better paid jobs;
- to provide the base data for the design or redesign of a pay structure;
- to give you information on what 'across-the-board' or specific increases you may need to give to keep pace with market rates, ie maintain a competitive pay structure.

How do you do all these things? First it is necessary to understand the concept of a market rate. You can then:

- identify sources of data
- obtain the data
- analyse the data
- use the data to provide guidance on decisions about levels of pay or pay increases.

What *is* a market rate?

You may not think that this is a sensible question. Everyone, you may say, knows what market rates are. But it is not quite as simple as that. Try answering these questions.

1. You look at job advertisements for product managers in *Campaign*. You find four jobs advertised in the last three issues which seem similar to your own job. They state salaries as:

- c (about) £20,000 plus car
- starting at £22,500, plus car
- £25,000, plus car
- c £27,500 (no mention is made of a car).

So what is the market rate?

2. You study various published salary surveys to find out what the market rate for a sales manager is. You look at the figures in three surveys for companies roughly the same size as your own. They are as follows:

	Lower quartile	Median	Upper quartile	No of companies
	£	£	£	
Survey A	27,500	33,000	40,000	19
Survey B	26,000	35,000	42,000	29
Survey C	23,000	29,000	34,000	56

What is the market rate for a sales manager?

3. One of your product managers has informed you that she has just got a job at £30,000 a year, plus a 2000cc car. She is at present on £25,000, plus a 1600cc car. The new job does not seem to be significantly different from her present one and, if anything, the company is less prosperous.

So, is the rate for the new job the market rate for product managers? And what do you do about your other product managers who are paid between £20,000 and £27,500 a year?

The answers to these questions are discussed in detail at the end of this chapter (pages 57–8), but in essence questions 1 and 2 indicate that you may not get precise information about market rates. Question 3 is a case where you have one example but can you really say that this is the market rate?

There is, in fact, seldom such a thing as *the* market rate. There is generally a range of market rates and you have to use judgement on what you think is the appropriate rate for the job in your company. The concept of the market rate is an inexact one. For example, if your company's policy is to pay at the upper quartile, which upper quartile do you choose in the example given above? You could average them, which would produce a figure of about £38,700 – but if you do this you will have committed the statistical sin of averaging averages, and the resulting figure has little relationship to reality.

Tick one only:

1. □ In the light of the above, I see no point in actively pursuing information on market rates. I am sure I can get a 'feel' for the rates without making a special effort.
2. □ The problem of getting information which tells you the exact market rate emphasises the need to track market rates systematically so that although you have to make a judgement, it is at least an informed one.

Many people subscribe to the beliefs expressed in comment 1. And indeed, it is possible to get a feel for the market by keeping your eyes open and your ear to the ground. But if you are having problems in recruiting or retaining people or if you feel your pay levels are slipping behind market rates, there is much to be said for taking a harder look at the market-place. As explained later, this will not necessarily take too much time or cost too much.

Other companies which are very conscious that they are

subject to market rate pressures do, however, subscribe to comment 2. They systematically track market rates using a selection of the sources mentioned below.

Where you stand will depend partly on the extent to which you believe you *are* subject to market pressures and the degree to which your policy aims to ensure that your levels of pay are competitive. Whatever approach you adopt, it is helpful to know the sources of data and how to obtain, analyse and use it as explained in the rest of this chapter.

Sources of market rate data

The main sources of market rate data are listed below. Indicate against each source the order in which you would place it compared with the others in terms of (a) the accuracy of the information and (b) the likely time and cost of obtaining the information (mark the most accurate type of information or the least time and cost as 1, the next most accurate or least time and cost as 2 etc).

	Accuracy	**Time and costs**
• Published surveys		
• Special surveys conducted by or on behalf of the company		
• Advertisements		
• Analysis of the details of pay given by applicants to jobs		
• Analysis of the pay existing employees get in new jobs		
• Informal or semi-formal exchange of views with managers from other companies		

	Accuracy	**Time and costs**
• 'Club data' – information collected and exchanged regularly by a group of companies which have formed a 'salary/pay club' for this purpose		
• Information on rates of pay or settlements published in journals such as *Incomes Data Services* or *Industrial Relations Services*		
• Information from trade associations and their journals.		

Detailed comments on the accuracy and cost of these sources are given in the Answers section on pages 58–9.

Generally speaking, however, surveys will provide the most accurate information in a systematic form, but the other sources can all be used without too much time or trouble although their accuracy is often suspect. The best approach is to collect data from as many sources as you can afford to use (in terms of both time and cost).

Obtaining data

When obtaining market rate data you need to consider the following points:

- The extent to which data is being obtained are similar to yours (called 'job matching') – obviously your aim is to compare like with like.
- The number of companies and jobs for which information is available – clearly, the more the merrier.
- The date of the survey – the more recent the better, otherwise you will have to make adjustments for possible increases since the survey took place.

Published surveys
Published surveys provide a lot of detailed information about rates of pay, bonus earnings and employee benefits. They may be general surveys for managers or they may be concerned with special occupational groups such as computer staff.

Published surveys can be quite expensive, although the more popular ones may be available for inspection in some libraries (eg the library of the Institute of Personnel and Development). They vary in the degree to which you can match your jobs accurately with theirs. They may produce 'capsule' job descriptions or indications of levels but precise matching is impossible.

Publications such as *Incomes Data Services* and *Industrial Relations Services* provide useful information on pay settlements and rates of increase. The names and addresses of the publishers of a selection of the main surveys are given on page 122.

Special surveys
You can carry out your own special survey or, at some expense, get management consultants to do it for you. This means that you can approach companies which are similar to yours and get information on specialised jobs which may not be available in the published surveys.

To conduct a special survey you have to write to a number of companies asking if they will exchange information with you and the other companies who may participate in the survey on the pay and benefits for specified jobs.

The quid pro quo for the companies who give you the information is that they get market rate data for free. This is normally issued on an anonymous basis and you have to promise complete confidentiality.

It is best to circulate a standard form on which pay data can be entered and brief 'capsule' descriptions of the jobs to be covered to help achieve good matching.

Companies will respond to such requests if they think they will get something out of it and if you create the right impression of professionalism in your approach to them. But many firms will not bother to answer, especially if they already take part in other surveys. As a result you may get an inadequate response – and you should aim for at least ten participants.

Salary clubs
A salary club is a group of companies which regularly exchange information about pay for specified jobs. This is a very good source of information if you can join such a club (ask around, but membership may be limited). You can set up your own club, possibly after running a special survey by inviting the participants to continue exchanging information on a regular basis. You will have to spend time in running the survey or get members to conduct it in turn, and it can be a time-consuming process. Alternatively, you can pay a management consultant to administer the survey for you and share the cost among club members.

Advertisements
For obvious reasons, advertisements are the most used source of market rate data. While there may not be such a thing as *the* market rate, people still gain an impression of what their personal market worth is through studying the situations vacant columns. You must therefore take account of advertisements. But be warned; the data can be misleading. It may be difficult to match jobs and quoted salaries, or rates of pay can be exaggerated by unscrupulous employers who want to attract a good field of candidates. 'Salary circa £x' can mean what is says – somewhere around, but it is often much lower.

Other sources
Other sources such as applicants, leavers and informal contacts can provide useful supplementary information, but should not be relied on.

Analysing market rate data
Published, special and club surveys will usually present their

data on basic pay or earnings (ie base pay plus bonuses) in the form of a statement of the lower quartile, median and upper quartile figures. They sometimes quote the whole range from top to bottom.

If you are seriously concerned with tracking market rates you need to collect information from as many sources as possible. It is then purely a matter of judgement as to what you assume to be the average rates with which you should compare your own pay levels. Averaging averages is a highly dubious statistical method but you may have to make general assumptions about what you believe to be a 'derived market rate'. The derivation of such a rate would not only be the actual figures from each source but also your own interpretation of the accuracy or significance of those figures.

Using market rate data

Market rate data provides guidance on the rate for a job or the 'going rate' (the latter is often defined as the general level of cost-of-living or negotiated increases). It can therefore be used to fix starting salaries, adjust scales, and indicate what general or specific market rate increases are available.

Answers

What is a market rate? (pages 51–2)

1. This is a fairly typical set of figures. You could take an average of, say, about £24,000 but this could be very misleading. It all depends on the degree to which the job advertised is similar to (matches) your job. All you could probably say is that you have to think in terms of a range from £20,000 to £27,500. You might settle for a figure of, possibly, £25,000, if this fits in with your existing rates and if the job advertised at that figure looks like yours.

2. This a good example of the sort of dispersion in figures you typically get when you study a number of surveys. All you

can do is to exercise judgement along the lines suggested earlier in producing a 'derived' market rate.

3. The new rate is what another company thinks it is worth paying your product manager. It therefore represents what they think is her personal market worth. It is certainly not the market rate and you should not take panic measures to increase the salaries of all your other product managers. But it would be a good idea to carry out a reasonably systematic survey of market rates for product managers and make any adjustments to the salaries of your own people if the survey indicates that they are falling behind *and* if you are anxious to retain them.

Accuracy and cost of market rate data sources (pages 53–4)
Generally, the relative accuracy and cost of sources is as follows:

	Accuracy	Time and costs
● Published surveys	3	2
● Special surveys conducted by or on behalf of the company	2	1
● Advertisements	9	7
● Analysis of the details of pay given by applicants to jobs	7	6
● Analysis of the pay existing employees get in new jobs	8	8
● Informal or semi-formal exchange of views with managers from other companies	6	9
● 'Club data' – information collected and exchanged regularly by a group of companies which have formed a 'salary/pay club' for this purpose	1	3

	Accuracy	Time and costs
• Information on rates of pay or settlements published in journals such as *Incomes Data Services* or *Industrial Relations Services*	5	4
• Information from trade associations and their journals.	4	5

CHAPTER 6
Job Evaluation

Market rate information provides information on external relativities. But you also need to know about internal relativities – the worth of one job compared with another inside the organisation and the differentials that should exist between them. These differentials are established by reference to this relative worth and are expressed in gradings and rates of pay for the various levels of jobs in an organisation.

Job evaluation defined

Job evaluation can be defined as the process of assessing the relative size of jobs within an organisation. In job evaluation terminology, the word 'size' is used to indicate the contribution made by the job to achieving the purpose of the organisation or part of the organisation. It covers the levels of skill and responsibility involved, the complexity of the job, the degree to which job holders have to exercise judgement in making independent decisions, and the size of the resources controlled in terms of the number of people managed, the size of the budget, or the size or value of the establishment or plant. Other significant dimensions which directly affect relative value include the sales turnover, contribution, added value or profit for which the job holder is accountable.

Job evaluation is essentially a comparative process. It deals with relationships not absolutes. There is no single unit of measurement which tells us precisely how much a job is worth. All we can do is compare the size of one job with another.

Why have job evaluation?

In one sense this is not a proper question. Whether you recognise the fact or not, you are evaluating a job every time you decide how it should be graded or what the rate of pay should be compared with other jobs in the company.

The real question is: do we need to adopt a formal approach to job evaluation? Here are some reasons for having a formal evaluation scheme. Assess their relative importance (1 is the most important etc). If you think they are irrelevant, indicate this with a 0.

Job Evaluation   **Order of importance**

a   Provides a rational basis for
    making defensible decisions on
    relativities
b   Indicates the correct rate of pay
    for jobs
c   Can, if properly managed,
    convince people that jobs are
    graded fairly
d   Ensures that 'equal pay for work
    of equal value' issues can be
    resolved satisfactorily
e   Tells you specifically what the
    value of a job is
f   Provides the information required
    to develop a logical and equitable
    pay structure
g   Enables internal relativities to be
    managed properly
h   Helps in decisions on how to

reconcile external and internal
relativities (ie situations when
market rate pressures upset
predetermined relativities within
the company).

Detailed comments on these benefits are made in the answers section at the end of the chapter (page 70). Suffice it to say at this stage that all of them are valid except the suggestion that job evaluation tells you what jobs should be paid. It cannot do that because there are so many other factors, including market rates and the impossibility of producing a formula which directly translates job evaluation judgements into money.

Do you need formal job evaluation?

Tick one only:

1. ☐ The advantages of job evaluation set out above can only be achieved if a formal systematic, and preferably analytical, system is used.
2. ☐ It is perfectly possible to make correct judgements about relative job values without going through all the largely spurious procedures involved in a formal job evaluation scheme.

Those who support formal, preferably analytical, job evaluation (option 1) do so because:

- It is systematic and analytical – it does not rely on possibly prejudiced and subjective judgements.
- It is, or should be, an open process – everyone can be informed about how decisions on the relative position of their job in a hierarchy have been made; it is not a 'behind closed doors' decision.
- It at least gives the appearance of objectivity (although most people admit that some subjectivity creeps in when making job evaluations).

- It is the only way to ensure that equal pay for work of equal value claims do not succeed (more about this later in this chapter).

Those who oppose the idea of formal evaluation say that:

- It is not really objective at all – the paraphernalia of factors, level definitions and points associated with analytical schemes as described later in this chapter do not alter the fact that in the last analysis job evaluation boils down to organised rationalisation.
- Formal job evaluation schemes cannot cope with new types of organisation or with 'knowledge workers' – they impose rigidity and create hierarchies which are out of place in flatter, flexible firms with people whose contribution largely depends on their individual skills and competences.
- All formal job evaluation schemes deteriorate over time and they can all be manipulated to produce whatever answers the evaluators want.
- They do not really indicate how jobs should be graded – all they do is put jobs in a hierarchy; judgement has still to be exercised on how they should be slotted into grades.
- They create unnecessary difficulties when it is found that external market rate pressures have to override internal relativities – and this happens frequently.
- They are expensive and time-consuming to introduce and operate.

The arguments for and against job evaluation seem to be equally convincing. What clinches the argument in favour of formal, analytical methods to many people is that they are at least systematic, open and logical, and they are essential as a means of dealing with equal pay issues.

The next four sections of this chapter therefore concentrate on formal job evaluation schemes, dealing with:

- Different types of scheme
- Job evaluation programmes

- Job analysis for evaluation
- The process of job evaluation.

Because many companies reject the idea of a formal, elaborate job evaluation scheme, the final section considers what approaches they can adopt to deal less formally with the management of relativities.

Types of job evaluation scheme

Job evaluation schemes can be divided into two categories:

- Non-analytical schemes which look at 'the whole job' and compare one job with another or with a grade definition — these comprise job ranking or job classification schemes.
- Analytical schemes which consider the different factors which contribute to job size and consider each of these separately — by far the most common form of analytical job valuation is the points scheme, often called point-factor rating.

Non-analytical schemes
Ranking schemes simply place jobs in rank order by looking at their relative size. They are crude and give no indication at all of how jobs should be graded.

Job classification schemes are based on definitions of grades in terms of the levels of responsibility, knowledge and skills and decision-making required of jobs in the grade. Jobs are slotted into grades by comparing the job description with the grade definition. These schemes are also pretty crude but they do settle grading decisions even if considerable judgement has to be used in the grade allocation process.

Point-factor rating (points schemes)
The analytical method of point-factor rating is based on the breaking down of jobs into elements common to all jobs. The key elements are identified as the factors which it is believed

contribute to differentiating the internal values of jobs in the organisation. This is called the factor plan. Typical factors include:

- Knowledge and skills
- Responsibility
- Decisions
- Complexity
- Contacts.

Definitions are produced for each of these factors. For example, complexity may be defined as: 'the variety and diversity of the tasks carried out by the job holder and the diversity of skills used'.

A total points score is then allocated to each factor. This score may be 'weighted' in accordance with a judgement of the relative significance of the factors. For example, the total points for the five factors mentioned above may be determined as follows:

• Knowledge and skills	120
• Responsibility	120
• Decisions	90
• Complexity	60
• Contacts	60

Each of the factors is divided into levels (usually four to six) representing the degree to which the factor is present in the job.

The next step is to define each level; for example, the lowest level for complexity may be defined as: 'Highly repetitive work where the same task or group of tasks is carried out without any significant variation'.

Finally, a points score or range is allocated to each level. A complete factor plan would look like this:

Factor	Levels					
	1	*2*	*3*	*4*	*5*	*6*
Knowledge and skills	20	40	60	80	100	120
Responsibility	20	40	60	80	100	120
Decisions	15	30	45	60	75	90
Complexity	10	20	30	40	50	60
Contacts	10	20	30	40	50	60

A factor plan

The job evaluation process involves analysing a job in terms of the factors, comparing that analysis with the factor and level definitions, allocating a level and score for each factor, and then adding up the factor scores to produce a total job evaluation score for the job. For example:

	Level	Score
Knowledge and skills	3	60
Responsibility	4	80
Decisions	4	60
Complexity	5	50
Contacts	3	30
Total score		280

The point scores can then be used to determine how the job should be allocated to grades which have been defined in terms of points. Thus, in this example, if the range for a grade were 250–300, the job would be allocated to that grade.

Point-factor schemes are by far the most popular, either in the form of tailor-made schemes for companies or the job evaluation packages — 'the proprietary brands' supplied by consultants such as Hay Management Consultants and the Wyatt Corporation. Although points schemes seem to be complex they are easy to use once evaluators have had some practice; a well-trained evaluation panel can reach consensus on the appropriate scores with remarkable ease. Point-factor schemes are therefore both credible and acceptable and they can be used effectively to deal with equal pay for work of equal value issues.

Job evaluation programme

A typical job evaluation programme consists of the following stages:

1. Decide in general what sort of scheme you want (for example, a points scheme) and whether you want to do it yourself or with outside help from consultants (their professional advice may be invaluable if you have had no experience in developing a job evaluation scheme).
2. Appoint a job evaluation panel of, say, six to eight members, ideally consisting of both managers and employee representatives.
3. Brief the panel and involve them in selecting and designing the scheme, assuming you are going to develop your own points scheme, with or without help.
4. Select a number of representative jobs (not too many) covering the major functions and occupations and levels of jobs in the organisation. These are the 'benchmark' jobs which provide the points of comparison for the evaluation process.
5. Analyse the benchmark jobs in terms of the factor plan (job analysis methods are described in the next section of this chapter).
6. Evaluate the benchmark jobs. This is done by the panel as a whole with someone – often a consultant or the personnel manager – acting as a facilitator. The aim should be to reach consensus and the panel will find it easier to do this under the guidance of a good facilitator, and easier still as members gain experience in using the scheme. It should be emphasised that their task is to evaluate the job, not the person doing the job. In other words the level of performance of job holders and their personal characteristics should not enter into the evaluation in any way.

7. Use the scores of the benchmark jobs to develop an initial grade structure defined in terms of point brackets. Clusters of point scores give some indication of which jobs naturally group together. To a degree, this will be a matter of judgement – the distribution of points will give some guidance, but ultimately everyone concerned has to feel that the grouping of jobs into grades is appropriate and fair. This is easily achievable when there is a clear hierarchy of jobs but difficulties can arise with borderline cases. The aim is to ensure that there is enough difference between the benchmark jobs in adjacent grades as indicated by the job analysis and evaluation to ensure that the allocation of the remaining jobs to those grades will not present any real problems.

8. Analyse and evaluate the remaining non-benchmark jobs and place them in grades.

You will then have a complete grade structure but you will not have established the pay ranges appropriate for each grade. This is done at the pay structure design stage as described in the next chapter.

Job analysis

The foundation of a reasonably objective job evaluation process is systematic job analysis. This applies particularly when you are conducting a formal exercise such as that described above. But even informal evaluation processes such as those considered in the next section will be more accurate if they are based on job analysis.

Job analysis gets the facts about the job from job holders and the job holders' managers. These facts are set out in a job description which:

- defines the overall purpose of the job in one sentence
- defines each of the main areas of responsibility (which may be termed principal accountabilities, main tasks or key result areas) – there should not be more than about ten areas, each

of which is defined in one sentence beginning with an active verb (eg prepare, produce, plan, ensure) and indicates what the job holder is required to do and achieve, not *how* it is done
- provides any additional background data on the nature and scope of the job; for example, the 'critical dimensions' of output or responsibility for people and budgets
- analyses the job in terms of each of the factors used in the evaluation scheme.

Less formal approaches to job evaluation

Less formal approaches to job evaluation are best based on some form of job analysis as described above if only to ensure that judgements are based on facts not opinions.

Informal decisions made on internal relativities can then be made, in effect, on a whole job comparison basis. The existing organisational hierarchy will provide a clear guide to the levels of responsibility that should be catered for in the grade structure, although the present hierarchy should not be taken as read. Job evaluation exercises can usefully serve as the basis for analysing organisation structures and job analyses can indicate any superfluous layers which might exist.

Information on market rate differentials can provide additional guidance on internal relativities. In many organisations a process of 'market pricing' is used which determines the whole pay structure by reference to market rates.

Conclusions

On the basis of what you have read in this chapter and your own experiences in this area, indicate whether you agree or disagree with the following statements (my comments are on page 71):

1. Formal job evaluation methods, especially
   points schemes, are fully objective.   ....
2. Ultimately, the effectiveness of job evaluation
   depends on the quality of the job analysis.   ....

3. Job evaluation clearly indicates how jobs should be graded.   ....

4. To be 'felt fair' by all concerned, employee representatives should be involved in the job analysis process.   ....

5. Individuals should be allowed to appeal against grading decisions made on the basis of job evaluation.   ....

6. Market rate data cannot be ignored when valuing jobs.   ....

7. While it is correct to say that you should not let the individual's performance in the job to affect the evaluation, it is also true that in some more flexible and/or highly responsible jobs, what is actually done can depend largely on the experience, knowledge, skills and competence levels of the job holder.   ....

Answers

Why have job evaluation? (pages 61–2)
The order of importance the writer would give is as follows:

1. (a)
2. (g)
3. (e)
4. (c)
5. (d)
6. (h)

Job evaluation does *not* by itself indicate the correct rate – the precise value – of a job. If you use a points scheme you cannot 'convert points to pounds'; there are too many other factors involved, especially market rate pressures. It can, however, compare the relative internal value or size of jobs so that they can be placed appropriately in a job hierarchy.

Conclusions – statements about job evaluation (pages 69–70)

1. No job evaluation scheme, even points, is fully objective. Judgement has still to be used in interpreting job analyses and relating these to factor definitions.
2. True, the foundation of all good evaluation is the factual analysis of jobs.
3. Not so: job evaluation will give *some* indication but there are often borderline cases at the boundaries of grades where judgement has to be used.
4. Involvement of employees is essential if the scheme is to achieve its objective of being felt to be fair and equitable.
5. An appeal process should be built into all job evaluation schemes.
6. If you use the term 'valuing jobs' in its widest sense, to mean deciding on the rate for the job, then market rate considerations have to be taken into account as well as internal relativities. How any conflict between these two influences can be dealt with is discussed in the next chapter.
7. In practice, in the sort of jobs mentioned in the last part of this comment, the individual's abilities and capacities *do* influence the size and scope of the job. This is why some organisations are developing skill/competence-based pay schemes as described in the next chapter in which, in effect, skill or competence is being used as a single job evaluation factor.

CHAPTER 7
Pay Structures

A pay structure consists of an organisation's pay ranges, either for jobs grouped into grades or for individual jobs, pay curves for job families, or pay scales for jobs slotted into a pay spine. However, a system of individual job rates (spot rates) could also be called a pay structure.

Purposes of pay structure

The purposes of pay structures are to:

- give a fair and consistent basis for motivating and rewarding employees
- provide a logically designed framework within which internally equitable and externally competitive pay policies can be implemented
- help in the management of relativities
- enable the organisation to recognize and reward people appropriately according to their job size, contribution, skill and competence.

Criteria for pay structures

Place the following criteria for pay structures in order of importance (1 for most important etc).

1. Fit the character and culture of the organisation.   ....
2. Enable the organisation to control the implementation of pay policies and budgets.   ....
3. Help to ensure that consistent decisions are made on pay.   ....
4. Be flexible in response to external (market) and internal (organisational change) pressures.   ....
5. Clarify pay and development opportunities and career ladders.   ....
6. Facilitate rewards for performance and achievement.   ....
7. Be constructed logically and clearly.   ....
8. Facilitate operational and job flexibility.   ....

These criteria can be summarised under four key headings:

- logical and fair
- manageable
- flexible
- facilitate rewards.

A suggested order for them is given on pages 83–4.

Types of pay structure

The main types of pay structure considered in this chapter are:

- graded structures
- pay spines
- pay curves
- spot rates.

Graded pay structures

A graded pay structure consists of a sequence of job grades, each of which is attached to a pay range. A typical graded structure with overlapping pay ranges is illustrated in Figure 7.1.

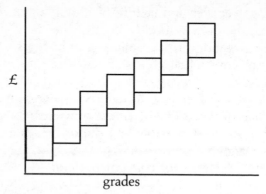

Figure 7.1 *A typical graded pay structure*

Main features of graded pay structures

The main features of graded pay structures are described below.

Job grades. Jobs are allocated to grades on the basis of an assessment of their relative size. If a points scheme is used this will be within a defined points range. All jobs in a grade are treated the same for pay purposes even if their job evaluation scores within the range are different.

Pay ranges are attached to each grade which define the minimum and maximum rate payable to any job in the grade, thus indicating the scope for job holders to progress through the range. A range can be defined in terms of the percentage increase between the lowest and highest point in the range, eg:

Minimum	Maximum	Range
£20,000	£26,000	30%

Alternatively, it can be defined as a percentage of the midpoint, eg:

Minimum	Midpoint	Maximum
£22,500	£25,000	£27,500
90%	100%	110%

Range reference points are incorporated in each range. They:

- indicate what the organisation is prepared to pay a fully qualified and competent individual
- are aligned to market rates in accordance with market rate policy, eg if the policy is to match market rates, then the reference point will represent the estimated average (median) market rates for the jobs in the grade.

The reference point is often at the midpoint of the range, the assumption being that an individual will progress to that point over a period of time. Experienced and capable individuals may be promoted or recruited to the grade anywhere between the bottom of the range and the reference point depending on their previous levels of experience and competence.

Differentials are provided between adjacent ranges which provide sufficient scope for recognising differences in the value of jobs between the grades concerned. Differentials tend to be between 15 and 20 per cent.

Overlap between grades is often a feature of graded salary structures. It is measured by the proportion of a range which is covered by the next lower range. For an organisation with a wide variety of jobs where a reasonable degree of flexibility is required in grading, the overlap may be as much as 50 per cent as in the following example.

Grade A	Grade B	Overlap
£12,000–£18,000	£14,400–£21,600	50%

Overlap allows organisations to recognise that a highly experienced person in a lower grade may be worth more than an inexperienced person in the next higher grade. It also addresses the problem of borderline grading decisions by reducing the differentials between adjacent grades.

Progression through grades may be achieved by fixed increments. However, in the private sector, at least, it is much more common nowadays for progression to be dependent on performance, ie through a performance-related pay (PRP) scheme. This is illustrated in Figure 7.2.

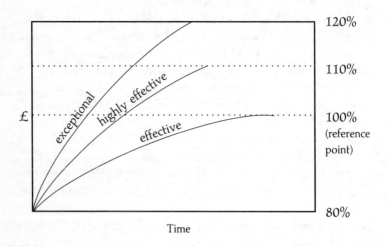

Figure 7.2 *Pay progression to varying target levels according to performance*

Make-up of a pay range. A typical make-up of a pay range into a series of zones is illustrated in Figure 7.3. The three zones are:

- *The learning zone* which represents the learning curve for inexperienced individuals beginning at the minimum rate of pay for the range.
- *The competent zone* which represents the range of pay for those who are competent in the key areas of their jobs.
- *The premium zone* which is reserved for individuals whose performance is exceptional, have acquired additional competences or who have special responsibilities which are higher than those carried out by others in the same grade but are not high enough to justify allocating the job into the next highest grade.

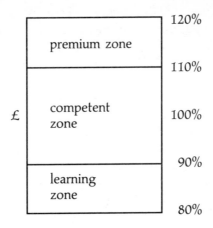

Figure 7.3 *Make-up of a pay range*

The number of grades will depend on the range of pay to be covered by the structure and the width of the grades. A typical structure ranging from £10,000 to £40,000 with medium width grades (say, 25 per cent) might have 12 or so grades. A 'broad-banded' structure with grades of 50 per cent or more might have considerably fewer grades – as little as four or five.

Progression through the structure will be based on promotion or on upgrading when the size of a job carried out by a job holder increases sufficiently on a permanent basis to place it in a higher grade. Care has to be taken to prevent 'grade drift' – unjustifiable upgrading resulting from pressures made by employees or their managers and engineered by manipulating the job evaluation systems.

Adjusting to allow for market rate pressures – on the basis of job evaluation alone (internal equity) a job may be placed in a particular grade. But market pressures may mean that individuals in that job have to be paid a rate higher than the scale for their grade. In these circumstances it is necessary to pay those individuals a market premium on their grade pay scale. They should not be placed in a higher grade as this would destroy the integrity of the grade structure.

This process is sometimes called 'red-circling' to indicate that these individuals are special cases. The term red-circling is also used when for historical reasons individuals are paid more than their job evaluated grade would justify.

Number of structures. Most organisations have one structure to cover all managerial, supervisory, professional, technical and office staff, sometimes excluding directors. Works employees are usually treated differently, generally being paid on a spot rate system plus, as described later in this chapter, incentive pay in many cases. However, more organisations are now introducing integrated graded structures covering all employees.

In organisations which employ large numbers of employees with high market rates (eg computer specialists), separate 'market group' structures may be created for them. This principle may be extended to job family structures in a pay curve system as described later in this chapter.

Designing graded structures

Graded structures are designed or modified initially on the basis of a job evaluation exercise which, if a points scheme is used, indicates the points ranges for each grade.

The design has to take into account the company's policy on the width of grades. If a flexible approach is necessary a broad-banded system will be preferred with a fairly wide range of jobs in each grade. If a more tightly controlled structure is required fairly narrow bands will be preferred; this approach allows for greater precision but encourages grade drift. The broad-banded system allows for greater flexibility but can cost more unless careful control is exercised to prevent everyone drifting up to the top of the band, irrespective of merit.

The structure must also take account of market rates in accordance with the company's market rate policy or 'pay stance'. The problem here is the imprecise nature of market rates, as mentioned in Chapter 5, and the requirement to exercise judgement on how these imprecise rates should be related to the group of jobs allocated to a range by job evaluation. The range of market rates may, however, give some indication of the desirable width of the salary scale for the grade. If some jobs with high market rates cannot be accommodated in the range they may have to be given a market premium and 'red circled'.

The problem in designing or modifying pay structures is that of reconciling the mix of considerations to be taken into account, ie job evaluation scores, market rate data and the policy of the company on flexibility or control and the width of grades (broad or narrow banding). Due to the difficulty of reconciling these often conflicting requirements, the process of a pay structure design is not a particularly scientific one. It is often an iterative process − one of trial and error − which involves producing a structure design and then having to go back to the drawing board to try an alternative which produces a better solution. Structure designers can be helped in this somewhat tedious process by special computer software which enables them to try out different solutions on a 'what if' basis.

Advantages and disadvantages of graded structures

The advantages of graded structures in terms of logic, equity and manageability seem obvious, but there are disadvantages too. List below what appear to you to be the potential advantages and disadvantages of such structures.

_____	_____
_____	_____
_____	_____
_____	_____
_____	_____

Suggested answers are provided on pages 84–5.

Pay spines

Pay spines consist of a series of incremental points extending from the lowest to the highest paid jobs covered by the structure. Pay scales or ranges for different job grades are then superimposed on the spine. An illustration of a pay spine is given in Figure 7.4.

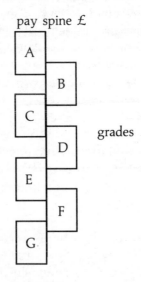

Figure 7.4 *A pay spine*

Pay spines are most often used in the public and voluntary sectors. If performance-related pay is introduced, individuals can be given accelerated increments. They are somewhat inflexible.

Pay curves

Pay curves, sometimes called maturity or progression curves, recognise that different methods of handling pay determination and progression may have to be used in different job families within which the nature of the work is similar, but the level at which the work is carried out is different, for example; design or development engineers, research scientists, accountants or personnel specialists.

Pay curves as illustrated in Figure 7.5 provide different pay progression tracks along which people in a family of jobs can move according to their levels of competence and performance. Pay levels are determined by reference to market rates.

The assumptions governing pay curves are:

- Competence develops progressively through various levels or bands rather than between a number of fixed points.
- Individuals will develop at different rates and will therefore deliver different levels of performance.
- Market rate considerations are likely to be important and should be taken into account when determining the levels of pay at each point in the curve.

Pay curves may be appropriate for job families consisting of 'knowledge workers' — scientists, technicians, professional staff

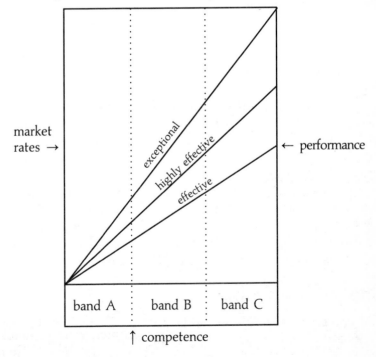

Figure 7.5 *A pay curve*

— whose importance to the organisation depends primarily on how they apply their knowledge, skills and competences and who cannot be slotted into a clearly defined hierarchy where the level is determined by managerial authority and the size of resources controlled. Pay curves are also more suitable in organisations which use project teams extensively.

The problem with pay curves is that they are harder to manage and less easy to control than graded pay structures. They will be unsuitable in a hierarchical organisation which operates in a bureaucratic manner and does not want to treat its various 'job families' differently.

Spot rates

A spot or individual job rate structure allocates a specific rate for a job. There is no defined pay range and how far the individual's pay rises above the rate, if at all, is at the discretion of management. Spot rate structures are typical for manual workers where the rates for skilled, semi-skilled and unskilled work may be fixed by negotiation. Spot rates for managers, professional and office staff are often used in fairly new organisations which have not got around to developing a formal graded structure. They are also adopted by managements who want to pay what they like and cannot be bothered with formal job evaluation to establish internal relativities or with predetermined pay ranges through which individuals' rates of pay can progress.

Spot rate structures can be based on formal job evaluation but, in most cases, pay levels are fixed by reference to market rates (market pricing) and will be heavily influenced by management's opinion of the market worth of individuals and how much they will contribute to the company.

Choice of structure

The choice of structure depends very much on the type of company and the kind of people the structure covers. What types of structures do you think you might find in the following companies?

1. A large, traditionally organised building society with clearly defined hierarchies and a somewhat autocratic management style.
2. A small but rapidly growing high-tech company employing highly qualified scientists in research and development projects and using a number of highly sophisticated project control techniques. A lot of attention is paid to developing the skills of employees. For example, the company is keen that its laboratory assistants should become qualified to undertake a full R & D role.
3. The organisation is a charity providing care for people with learning difficulties. Most of its care workers are recruited from local authority social services departments which pay National Joint Council scales.
4. This mail order company is small but growing rapidly. It needs to attract young people with good experience of direct mail marketing from similar organisations. The majority of its marketing staff are young, ambitious graduates who want to make a name for themselves in direct mail or advertising.
5. This is a medium-sized engineering company which negotiates rates of pay for manual workers with its trade union. Salaried staff in the well-established manufacturing, production engineering, design, marketing and administrative departments are covered by a separate pay structure which is not negotiated.

Suggestions on the sorts of structures you might find in these organisations are given on pages 85–6.

Answers

Criteria for pay structures (page 72)
The suggested order of importance is as follows:

1. Be constructed logically and clearly.
2. Help to ensure that consistent decisions are made on pay.

3. Fit the character and culture of the organisation.
4. Enable the organisation to control the implementation of pay policies and budgets.
5. Facilitate rewards for performance and achievement.
6. Be flexible in response to external (market) and internal (organisational change) pressures.
7. Facilitate operational and job flexibility.
8. Clarify pay and development opportunities and career ladders.

Advantages and disadvantages of graded structures (page 79)

Advantages

- Consistent methods of grading jobs and managers relativities are provided.
- A well-defined and comprehensible framework exists for managing reward and career progression.
- Relativities are clearly indicated and can be defended, especially if the structure is based on job evaluation.
- A broad-banded structure allows a degree of job flexibility and scope to accommodate differences between the market rates of jobs in the grade.
- Better control can be exercised over pay for new starters, individual performance-related pay increases and promotion increases.

Disadvantages

- The existence of grade boundaries dividing jobs into separate grades creates discontinuity and creates problems of 'boundary management', ie deciding which jobs fall into the higher or lower of two adjacent grades.
- There is often a tendency for grade drift as jobs get pushed unjustifiably into a higher grade as a result of pressure from employees and, frequently, their managers.
- Grouping jobs into grades inevitably means that the jobs in

a grade will be of different sizes. The smaller jobs in the grade may be over-paid while the larger jobs may be underpaid. To avoid this problem some companies introduce individual job grades for senior staff and work out relativities and salary levels on the basis of points scores.

- The existence of a range creates expectations among employees that they will inevitably reach the top even if it has been stressed that only people whose performance is exceptional will move into the highest 'premium' zone of a range. Managers often hate to disappoint their staff and therefore allow their pay to drift to the top of the range irrespective of their performance. It is in practice very difficult to halt someone's progression in a range.

- When staff do reach the top there is nowhere else for them to go unless they are promoted. Yet they will continue to make a good contribution and it is a pity if they are demotivated by not being able to go any further. What would you do if you were the manager in such a situation? (Suggested answer on page 86.)

Choice of structure (page 83)

1. The most likely structure will be a graded one with fairly narrow bands and, possibly, fixed incremental scales through each grade, especially for more junior jobs.

2. This is the ideal situation for a pay curve system which relates progression to the achievement of defined competence levels.

3. Most of the staff of the charity, and also many of its trustees, are likely to have had experience in local authorities where pay spines are the most common form of structure. The fact that staff are being recruited from local authorities, many of whom pay National Joint Council rates, will make it even more probable that a pay spine will be used. It is most unlikely that pay will be related to performance in any way.

4. This sort of company will almost certainly have a spot rate structure, although they would not call it that. Manage-

ment will pay people what it needs to attract them from other firms and, if they are any good, will give them increases which will ensure that they are unlikely to be poached, at least for a year or so. It is known broadly what staff will be paid within some sort of limit – secretaries, for example, between £12,000 and £14,000 and product managers between £21,000 and £30,000. But there is plenty of flexibility to pay more or less than these understood, although not defined, limits.

5. The manual workers will be on the negotiated rate for the job, in effect a spot rate. This may be a 'high day rate' or they may be in an incentive scheme. Staff are likely to be placed in a graded salary structure, probably based on job evaluation.

What to do about people who hit the ceiling (page 85)

One method which many companies adopt to get out of this impasse is to make achievement bonuses available to those at the top of their scale. These would only be paid if the individual has made an exceptional contribution; they would not be handed out as a matter of course.

CHAPTER 8
Performance-related Pay

Pay systems start by establishing the rate for the job on the basis of market rate surveys, job evaluation and, sometimes, trade union negotiations. These determine the pay structure. If the policy of the organisation is to make individual differential payments according to performance, skill or competence, the pay structure will be designed as we saw in Chapter 7 to allow for these additional elements of remuneration. The pay system may also incorporate organisation-wide schemes for rewarding employees generally according to the performance of the business.

This chapter is mainly concerned with the most common form of differential payment for staff – performance-related pay (PRP). But it also deals briefly with profit-related pay which, confusingly, is often also termed PRP.

Performance-related pay: general considerations

Tick one only:

1. ☐ I believe that it is absolutely right for people to be rewarded according to their performance, and doing so will significantly increase their motivation and their added-value contribution.

2. ☐ I dislike the whole idea of paying for performance because it is often fundamentally unfair and even when it is functioning fairly, there is no evidence that any but the crudest piecework incentive schemes do actually motivate people to perform significantly better.

If you have ticked (1) read on – this chapter is for you. If you have ticked (2) still read on. At least you should be aware of the arguments for and against performance-related pay and how it can be made to work in some circumstances.

Why have performance-related pay?

Advocates of performance-related pay claim that it enables an organisation to:

- establish a clear relationship between performance and pay
- provide the most direct and meaningful form of financial motivation available by linking rewards to achievements
- concentrate effort in priority areas
- clarify the key issues with which employees should be concerned
- attract and retain people who are confident in their ability to deliver results but expect to be rewarded accordingly
- improve pay competitiveness
- enable employees to share in the success of the company if pay-offs are related to business performance, eg profits, added value.

The following are some statements frequently made about performance-related pay. Indicate whether, in your opinion, they are true or false.

True   False

1. It is right and proper that people should be rewarded individually according to their contribution.   ____ ____

2. Performance-related pay (PRP) is the best way of motivating employees.   ____ ____

3. Shop floor incentive schemes always result in wage drift.   ____ ____

4. Wage drift can always be controlled by effective management.   ____ ____

5. Individual incentive or PRP schemes militate against good team work.   ____ ____

6. PRP is a good way of getting the message across – that performance matters.   ____ ____

7. Individual incentive schemes mean that workers tend to go for quantity rather than quality.   ____ ____

8. All PRP schemes are basically flawed because they depend on subjective ratings made by managers.   ____ ____

9. PRP schemes won't work as motivators because the link between performance and reward is insufficiently clear.   ____ ____

10. PRP schemes can provide the leverage necessary to develop a performance-orientated culture.   ____ ____

11. No research project has yet produced any evidence that PRP schemes can increase motivation and improve organisational performance.   ____ ____

12. Company-wide profit sharing schemes may increase commitment but are not effective as direct motivators.   ____ ____

Comments on each of these statements are given on pages 98–9.

Reservations about performance pay

The rationale for performance pay is powerful, but some people have reservations about it. The main objections are that:

- It is difficult to get it right and genuinely relate rewards to performance – the criteria for a successful performance-pay scheme as listed on page 91 are exacting.
- Staff in PRP schemes often believe that the ratings which determine rewards are unfair.
- By making pay contingent on performance (as judged by the firm) management is signalling that they are in total control – there is no room left for the intrinsic motivation that can result when staff are empowered to manage and control their jobs.
- Recent research in motivation has shown that intrinsic interest in a task – the sense that something is worth doing for its own sake – typically declines when someone is only given external reasons for doing it.
- Getting people to chase money can produce nothing except people chasing money – where does quality and customer service come in?
- A number of recent research projects have failed to establish any link between PRP and organisational performance – one of the studies carried out in 1993 by the Institute of Manpower Studies produced the conclusion that PRP 'fails to improve staff achievement and often leads to a downward spiral of demotivation'.

You may feel that some of these opinions are unrealistic and, in spite of the outcome of a number of research projects, you could still believe deep down from your own experience that performance pay is a good thing.

But the criteria as set out below for getting performance pay right are demanding, and there is no doubt that many organisations get them wrong. Too much money is squandered on PRP schemes that do not pay off.

Criteria for performance pay

PRP schemes need to be considered in terms of the following six golden rules:

1. Individuals and teams need to be clear about the targets and standards of performance required, whatever they may be.
2. They should be able to track performance against those targets and standards throughout the period over which performance is being assessed.
3. They must be in a position to influence the performance by changing their behaviour or decisions.
4. They should be clear about the rewards they will receive for achieving the required end results.
5. The rewards should be meaningful enough to make the efforts required worthwhile – and the communication of the rewards should be positively handled.
6. The formula should be simple and easy to understand.

Try these criteria on your own PRP scheme or one well known to you. How does it measure up against each criterion? If it fails in any *one* of them it is suspect. If it fails on two or three it is highly doubtful. If it fails on four or five criteria then it ought to be scrapped forthwith.

Arguments for and against PRP

Here are some of the arguments for and against PRP. Give those *for* PRP marks of zero to plus ten according to your assessment of their validity. Give those *against* PRP marks of zero to minus ten, again according to the extent to which you agree or disagree with them.

For **Rating**
0 to +10

A It is right and equitable to reward people
according to their contribution.
_____

For **Rating**
0 to +10

B PRP provides a tangible means of recognising achievement.

_____

C PRP ensures that everyone understands the performance imperatives of the organisation.

_____

D PRP works well as an incentive because money is the best motivator.

_____

E Because of its effectiveness as a motivator of individual performance, PRP can make a significant impact on the results obtained by the organisation.

_____

F PRP focuses the attention of individuals on the things that matter in their jobs.

_____

Against **Rating**
0 to −10

a The effectiveness of PRP as a motivator is questionable. There is little firm evidence that people are motivated by their expectations of the relatively small rewards they are likely to get (if they get them at all).

_____

b Financial incentives may work well for some people because their expectations that they will be rewarded are high, but such individuals will tend to be well-motivated anyway. Less confident employees will not respond so well to the possibility of rewards they do not expect to achieve.

_____

c It can be difficult to measure individual performance objectively. Unfair assessments are easily made in circumstances where ratings may well be both subjective and inconsistent. Even if this is not the case, employees may well *perceive* that this is what is happening. And this will demotivate them. _____

d PRP can encourage people to focus narrowly on the tasks that will earn brownie points and to be less concerned about longer-term issues, quality and innovation. _____

e If there is an undue emphasis on individual performance, teamwork will suffer. _____

f It can lead to pay drifting upwards without any commensurate improvement in performance. _____

The writer's own ratings are given on pages 99–100.

When analysing your ratings look first at the overall for and against scores. Whether they show that you are in favour of PRP or the reverse, look more carefully at your low marks on the positive points and your high marks on the negative points. Is there anything you can do, in the words of the old song, to 'eliminate the negative and accentuate the positive'? If you or your organisation are contemplating the introduction of PRP, these points are well worth considering. It is just as important to give them your attention if you already have PRP (whether you like it or not). You should want to capitalise on it, or at least make the best of a bad job.

How PRP works

PRP provides for variable performance-related payments to be made in a pay range. Progression within the range is determined by ratings of performance, eg:

A Outstanding performance in all respects
B Superior performance, significantly above normal job requirements
C Good all round performance which meets the normal requirements of the job

D Performance not fully up to requirements
E Unacceptable level of performance.

Guidelines would then be issued on what percentage increases to pay may be given for each rating level. These guidelines would be prepared on assumptions about the distribution of ratings and the amount of money available. For example, if the budget for PRP increases is 3.3 per cent of the payroll, the guidelines might look like this:

	Proportion of ratings	**% increase**
A	5	10
B	10	7
C	70	3
D	12	0
E	3	0

Within a range, guidelines might be prepared to illustrate the rate of progression people rated at different levels of performance could achieve if they receive consistent ratings. As illustrated in Figure 7.2 (page 76) these may take individuals so far up the range but no further unless their performance improves. Of course, in practice, ratings may not be consistent and progression will not necessarily follow the smooth lines given in the example.

Some companies are now paying achievement or sustained high levels of performance lump-sum bonuses as an alternative to a pay increment. The value of the bonus in percentage of salary terms may be the same as an increment for the same level of performance. In fairly rare cases such payments entirely replace increments so that individuals receive a reasonably high rate of pay (in line with their market worth) and receive additional bonuses as and when they are earned. In other cases they are used as alternatives to increments, for example when employees have reached the top of their pay range. A compromise practice is to pay performance-related increments while individuals are in their 'learning zone', ie until they are fully competent, and then only pay bonuses to those who deliver even higher levels of performance.

What makes a worthwhile reward?

To a degree, the answer to this question must be 'it all depends' – on the individual's needs and wants, on how much effort or risk is involved in obtaining the reward, on whether the incentive or bonus is just a 'top up' to a high base rate, and on the extent to which the reward is mainly treated as a tangible, possibly token, form of recognition.

The handouts in many performance-related pay schemes are fairly small – 3 to 5 per cent is fairly common. The extent to which rewards of this relatively insignificant size will motivate can be questioned. Are individuals really going to work harder throughout the year in the expectation that they *might* (there is no guarantee) get a 3 per cent increase to their salary?

Some organisations are now recognising that the proportion of differential pay should be much higher – 10 per cent upwards of total earnings – to provide a significant incentive or reward. But they may achieve this by holding base pay down and putting a greater proportion of earnings at risk. In other words, they are not making any 'new money' available. They are simply redistributing existing funds so that they can make a greater impact on individual and, importantly, team performance.

Team pay

PRP schemes generally provide rewards to individuals, but the increasing emphasis on teamwork in flatter and more flexible organisations means that many companies are introducing some form of team pay. This usually takes the form of a lump-sum cash bonus which is shared between team members if the team as a whole has achieved certain agreed targets.

Appropriateness of PRP

If you are contemplating introducing PRP you must consider whether or not your organisation is ready for it. If you already have PRP you need to review from time to time whether it is appropriate, in the sense that it is working well for you.

The following are a number of criteria for assessing whether PRP is appropriate. Against each criterion indicate from your knowledge of your own organisation whether the situation completely meets the criterion (score 2), partially meets the criterion (score 1), or totally fails to meet the criterion (score 0).

1. PRP does, or is likely to, fit and support the culture of the organisation.
2. PRP can act as a lever for changing the culture.
3. There is total clarity about what success looks like in the organisation.
4. There are fair and consistent methods available (or which can be made available) for measuring the performance of those who may be eligible for PRP.
5. There is a process of performance management incorporating individual objective-setting processes which can be used as the basis for performance rating.
6. Individual objectives agreed as part of the performance management process are integrated with functional/ departmental and business objectives.
7. Managers and team leaders are fully capable of measuring performance against objectives and providing feedback.
8. Managers and team leaders can translate their measurements of performance into fair and consistent ratings as a basis for performance-related pay-outs.
9. The organisation is prepared to spend time and money in training managers and team leaders to operate PRP, including the processes involved in measuring and rating performance.
10. The organisation has set clear and realistic objectives on what the PRP scheme should deliver in terms of improved motivation and performance.

11. The organisation is prepared to monitor and evaluate the performance of PRP against those objectives.
12. There are clear guidelines to managers on how the pay of employees performing at different levels should progress through the pay range for their grade.
13. Steps are taken to ensure that the application of these guidelines is monitored so that they are used fairly and consistently.
14. The organisation has set aside a sum of money for PRP which will ensure that worthwhile rewards are available to those who deserve them.
15. The PRP scheme ensures that performance priorities are highlighted.
16. These priorities include not only performance in terms of output or quantifiable contribution but also performance in less quantifiable but potentially equally significant areas such as quality, teamwork, innovation, the provision of safe and healthy systems of work, implementing equal opportunity policies and importantly, success in developing staff.
17. The communication systems of the organisation can effectively get the message across about the purpose of PRP and how it will benefit both the organisation and individuals.
18. The organisation is prepared to involve employees in developing and monitoring PRP.
19. There is unequivocal commitment to PRP on the part of top management.
20. Line managers support and 'own' PRP.
21. Employees generally accept that PRP is fair and that they benefit from it.
22. The trade unions (if any) actively support PRP.

These criteria can be used as guidelines on introducing and operating PRP. If your score is 40 or more you are either ready for PRP or you are operating it successfully. If your score is between 25 and 40 there are some areas which will need attention but if this is given, PRP can be made to work reasonably well. A score of between 10 and 25 means that you have serious problems. PRP could be made to function well but it will take a lot of work. If your score is less than 10 then there is not much hope for PRP in your organisation.

Profit-related pay

This is a UK government-sponsored scheme in which part of the pay of employees is related to company profits. Employees therefore receive a share of the profits they help to create. The key features of profit-related pay are:

- It provides for substantial tax relief if it meets stringent government conditions – profit-related pay is free of income tax up to a point when it is 20 per cent of total pay or £4,000 a year, whichever is lower (these sums are subject to alteration by the government).
- In most schemes part of pay is converted to profit-related pay – ie there is what is termed 'salary sacrifice'.
- Profit-related pay can go up or down with profits so that there is always a risk if salary has been sacrificed that employees will be worse off.

Answers

Statements about paying-for-performance (pages 88–9)

1. *True* – this statement ought to be self-evident; people should be paid according to their just deserts, ie what they contribute.
2. *False* – PRP can motivate people but it often fails to do so. Motivation is best achieved through an appropriate mix of financial and non-financial motivators.
3. *True* – no shop-floor scheme can avoid some measure of wage drift, although it can be controlled.
4. *False* – see above, management can control its effects but cannot abolish it.

5. *True* — up to a point. Individual schemes can hinder teamwork but it is possible to mitigate this effect by introducing effectiveness as a team member as one of the criteria for PRP.

6. *True* — as long as management makes a determined effort to get this message across; it will not penetrate by itself.

7. *True* — up to a point. It is possible to introduce quality considerations into the criteria for earning an incentive payment.

8. *True* — this is perhaps the most compelling objection to PRP, although if a PRP scheme is in operation efforts can and should be made to train managers in how to be objective and consistent with their ratings.

9. *True* — these are two of the fundamental flaws often built into PRP schemes. In fact, PRP can sometimes only be justified because it at least delivers a message about performance and provides some form of tangible recognition of achievement. The latter is indeed a motivator but not a particularly significant one.

10. *True* — this is perhaps the most powerful argument for PRP and in some organisations it can override all the objections to PRP as an inadequate motivator.

11. *True* — there have been many recent research projects but none has detected any direct link between PRP and company performance.

12. *True* — profit-sharing is too remote from the day-to-day concerns of employees to act as a direct incentive, although it can increase identification with, and therefore commitment to, the company. Gainsharing, however, can be used as a motivator.

Arguments for and against PRP (pages 91–3)

My ratings are plus (for PRP) 32 and minus (against PRP) 36. My experience of installing, operating and evaluating PRP and the evidence of research suggests that as a motivator it can often be a very dubious proposition. And it is very difficult to make it work well. However, I would be prepared to agree that in some circumstances PRP can be effective. My negative views are based on actual experience, but we can all learn from experience and if careful attention is paid to the criteria listed on page 91 of this chapter and the tips given below, it is possible to turn the negatives into positives.

Tips on making performance-related pay work

- Define objectives of PRP and the criteria for measuring its effectiveness.
- Consider piloting PRP so that improvements can be made in the light of experience.
- Involve employees in the preliminary discussions on the purpose of PRP, how it will work and how they will benefit from it.
- Communicate to employees the reason for PRP and how it functions. If you are running PRP as a pilot scheme, inform them accordingly, pointing out that you will be discussing how it worked with all concerned and may make amendments accordingly.
- Develop a performance management system which provides a basis for fair measurement of performance against agreed objectives and competence criteria.
- Design rating systems which do reflect the judgements made in performance reviews and can be used fairly and consistently by managers.
- Ensure that managers are trained in how to measure and rate performance and how to explain PRP to their staff.
- Ensure that managers convey to their staff the relationship between performance and reward and the basis upon which the decisions affecting the reward were made. These decisions should be clearly related to the performance management process which should involve employees in assessing their own performance so that the rationale behind ratings is more likely to be accepted as fair.
- Provide meaningful rewards, as long as you can afford them. If you cannot, you should question the use of PRP.
- Consider the use of lump-sum achievement or sustained

bonus payments which could be more meaningful than a minute percentage increase to base pay.

- Monitor the PRP awards to ensure that they are being made fairly and consistently.
- Evaluate the effectiveness of PRP against the objectives you set for it.
- Consider conducting an attitude survey to obtain employee reactions to PRP.
- Be prepared to amend the PRP system on the basis of evaluations and reactions.

CHAPTER 9

Managing Pay Systems – What Organisations Do

To manage their reward systems effectively organisations initially need to:

- develop reward strategies (see Chapter 4)
- formulate reward policies (see Chapter 4)
- survey market rates (see Chapter 5)
- evaluate jobs internally (see Chapter 6)
- develop and maintain pay structures (see Chapter 7)
- introduce performance-related pay schemes if their policy is to offer differential rewards (see Chapter 8).

Additionally they have to develop their policies on total remuneration (see below) and deal with the following aspects of managing the system (also dealt with in later sections of this chapter):

- deciding on the extent to which line managers are to be involved in running the system in their own areas
- maintaining communication with employees about the system
- developing a performance-management system
- introducing procedures for fixing rates of pay
- conducting individual pay reviews
- ensuring that value for money is obtained from the system.

Total remuneration

The concept of total remuneration involves treating all aspects of pay and benefits policy as a whole. It means assessing the best mix of the possible components of remuneration at each level. And these should be considered from the viewpoints of both the organisation and the staff.

The elements of total remuneration are:

- Basic pay, pensions, sick pay, holidays, employee share and other entitlements provided for all employees
- Benefits or additional remuneration which are only provided to certain employees, eg executive share options, company cars
- Benefits only provided for individual needs, eg housing and removal assistance.

The mix will need to be considered in the light of policies on differentials and comparisons with competitors.

Some companies are adopting a more flexible approach to total remuneration by offering employees a measure of choice in their benefits. This is sometimes called a 'cafeteria' or flexible benefit system, and enables them to choose from a range of options within the total remuneration sum. For example, a smaller car may be chosen and the money made available spent on other benefits.

Involvement of line managers

The basic philosophy of human resource management (HRM) is that all the processes involved in managing human resources should be owned and driven by line management. The human resource or personnel function is there to come up with good ideas about how best to manage human resources, but these ideas are implemented by line managers with whatever guidance and support they need from personnel. It may, however, be necessary to exercise some measure of functional control to ensure that personnel policy guidelines are implemented with a reasonable degree of consistency (although some flexibility is necessary).

Tick one only:

1. ☐ I believe that it is essential to devolve the maximum amount of authority to line managers to manage their own pay systems within their budgets and broadly in line with policy guidelines. After all, managers are fully accountable for the results and they should be trusted to deal responsibly with pay matters. If they cannot be trusted they should not be managers.

2. ☐ I think it is essential that management maintains full control over the reward system. If they leave it to individual managers you will get inconsistencies and inequities throughout the organisation. Favouritism will prevail and policy guidelines will be ignored.

If you tick (1) you are clearly someone who believes that organisations should be run on the basis of empowerment and trust. If you give managers authority to deal with pay matters, albeit within budgets and in accordance with guidelines, then you are empowering them and empowerment depends upon trust. This can be built up by treating managers as responsible human beings, not like children. Of course, you still have to ensure that managers receive the training they need to carry out their responsibilities, and support and guidance should be available to them as required. Many line managers like to be left alone to get on with things. Others want and appreciate help. Both types should be catered for.

If you tick (2) then you believe that pay is such a vital, and expensive, issue that full control has to be maintained over it from the centre. You are concerned with consistency, equity and order, and fear that with the best will in the world even trustworthy managers may still be unable to manage their reward systems to meet these essential requirements.

A balance may have to be struck between these two views. Empowerment is a good thing but empowerment without responsibility is dangerous. In this key area of management the centre has to take the responsibility for developing policy guidelines and ensuring that they are implemented. The issue may be the degree to which these guidelines are rigid. Organisations today have to operate much more flexibly than before and have to devolve decision-making as close to the scene of action as possible. This includes decisions on rates of pay for those joining the company or on promotion and decisions on individual pay increases. In both these cases, however, the decisions must be made within the manager's pay budget and in line with the pay structure and pay review policies.

Communicating with employees

One of the prime objectives of the pay system should be to motivate people and ensure their commitment. But how can the system motivate if left to its own devices – if people suspect that it is unfair, are unsure why it was developed in its present form, and do not really know how their pay is linked to performance or what their future rewards are going to be if they take on greater responsibility? These are aspects of the reward system which must be communicated to employees if the organisation is to get the maximum benefit from it.

Many companies are also now taking the view that employees tend to take for granted the various benefits provided for them, at considerable cost, by the company. They are therefore issuing employee benefit statements which spell out exactly what staff receive in terms of both pay and benefits, and the value of the latter to them.

Performance management systems

The essential components of a performance management system are that:

- The organisation has a shared vision of its objectives and a mission statement which it communicates to all its employees.

- Individual performance objectives and targets are agreed which are related both to operating unit and wider organisational objectives.
- Regular reviews of progress towards achieving these targets are conducted by managers with the individuals in their teams — these reviews may be formal or conducted informally throughout the year.
- The emphasis in these reviews is on conducting them as a dialogue about performance, progress and what needs to be done in the future.
- The reviews provide an opportunity for feedback, reinforcement and the recognition of achievements — they are therefore important vehicles for enabling managers to motivate people through non-financial rewards.
- The reviews are primarily forward-looking — spelling out future objectives and plans, planning for performance improvement and development and meeting training needs.

Performance management systems can therefore play a major part in the motivational processes. Essentially, they are tools for managers to use; they are not procedures like old-fashioned merit rating or performance appraisal schemes which were the creations of personnel departments and almost inevitably failed. Performance management must be owned both by managers and the individuals who are jointly concerned in the process with their bosses.

A performance management system can provide the fairest basis for determining performance-related pay awards because, if operated properly, it is objective and involves the joint agreement of progress, achievements and assessments.

Guidelines on fixing rates of pay

Policy guidelines should be prepared and communicated on:

- the procedures for grading or regrading jobs, making use of the job evaluation scheme
- fixing rates of pay on appointment — the policy should set

out the circumstances in which recruits can be paid above the minimum rate for the job or can be paid a special 'market' premium

- promotion increases – the guidelines should state what a meaningful increase would be, probably a minimum of 5 to 10 per cent.

Conducting general pay reviews

Tick one box only:

1. ☐ The organisation has the duty of protecting its employees against inflation. It must therefore award an annual 'across-the-board' cost-of-living increase in line with inflation over the previous year.

2. ☐ The organisation must maintain a competitive pay system which means adjusting rates either generally *or* for particular occupations in line with increases in market rates, which will be affected by inflation. But it cannot undertake to protect everyone's pay against increases in the cost of living. What happens if inflation goes up to 20 per cent a year or more as it did in the 1970s? Perhaps this will never happen again but the risk is there, and a business cannot afford to make any promises about linking pay to the cost of living. In any case, there may be some ineffective employees who do not deserve to have the purchasing power of their pay maintained. Why should they not have the real value of their pay reduced?

Most organisations still subscribe to the views expressed in (1). And it can be very difficult to move into the policy area defined in (2), especially if employees are used to cost-of-living increases.

Some organisations, however, are moving to a more flexible approach in line with (2). This says that they will not pursue a rigid cost-of-living policy. Instead, they will adjust their pay levels in line with increases in market rates. If they have a structure consisting of 'market groups' or 'job families' (see Chapter 7) they may flex the increase in accordance with differential market rate pressures.

Other organisations are going even further than this and are not conducting any general, separate pay reviews at all. Instead they review each employee's pay individually and award a total increase which takes account of performance, cost-of-living increases and market rate increases, ie increases in the 'market worth' of the individual. This gives them total flexibility but has to be controlled carefully as part of the individual pay review procedure as discussed below.

Individual pay reviews

If employees are not on incremental pay scales, which involve an automatic increase in pay every year, irrespective of performance, they will have to be reviewed individually, usually once a year.

In a PRP system as described in Chapter 8 this will involve producing guidelines on the percentage increases which can be given depending on performance and the overall pay review budget.

Organisations which do not believe in devolving too much to line managers will apply the guidelines rigidly, sometimes using a 'forced distribution' system which compels managers to distribute their ratings, and therefore their increases, in accordance with a distribution scale as in the example given on page 94.

This, of course, considerably reduces the amount of influence line managers have on pay and many organisations prefer to provide more general policy guidelines. These might, for example, state that the maximum award (except in very special circumstances) should be, say, 10 per cent and the minimum 3 per cent. A possible distribution between different levels of award would be suggested but it would be left entirely to the manager's discretion how they were distributed within the limits, as long as, importantly, managers do not exceed the budget for their payroll increase.

Getting value for money

Pay is almost always by far the highest item of expenditure of any organisation. It is therefore essential to get value for money from the pay system. How do you do this? Here are some suggestions. Rank them in order of importance (1 most important etc).

a Exercising strict control over all aspects of reward management
b Setting payroll budgets and ensuring that they are not exceeded
c Questioning every item of expenditure on employee benefits to ensure that they are worth while
d Not initiating any new approach to reward management (eg job evaluation, a new structure, PRP, or a cafeteria system) without carefully calculating its likely costs and benefits
e Monitoring and evaluating every aspect of reward management to ensure that the costs and benefits are all planned or projected.

A suggested rank order is given below but in practice all these factors are important and no business can afford to neglect any of them.

1 = b
2 = d
3 = e
4 = a
5 = c

CHAPTER 10
Reward Management – What Line Managers Do

Tick one only:

1. ☐ The impact line managers can make on motivation through pay is limited because normally they have little influence on the pay of their staff, which is determined by company policies and procedures.
2. ☐ Managers may not have much control over financial incentives and rewards but the equally, if not more, important motivation that can be achieved through non-financial incentives is almost entirely in their hands.

If you ticked (1) you are supporting a very common view which is entirely true in companies where rigid control is maintained over the reward system from the centre. One of the major contentions of this book is that such control is entirely inappropriate today when organisations have to operate much more flexibly and responsively to competition and customers' needs. These reactions are largely in the hands of line managers and if they are accountable for results they have to be given the tools for the job. In other words, they must be given the freedom to manage their human resources in a way which is most likely to bring about success. Of course, there are limits to all freedoms, including this one. There will be policy guidelines which line managers must apply and they have to work within the overall structure and strictly to budget. But within this framework they must be empowered to make their own decisions about their human resources.

If you ticked (2) you are subscribing to the belief that non-financial incentives are the key to long-term motivation, although it may well be advantageous to combine them in a total reward package with financial incentives.

Providing non-financial rewards

The non-financial rewards of achievement, recognition, responsibility, influence and personal growth are all under the control of line managers, especially when backed up by a performance-management system which operates in accordance with the principle 'managing performance throughout the year'.

If you are a line manager, every time someone carries out a special assignment for you this provides you with an opportunity to provide feedback and reinforcement if the individual has done well, and guidance, coaching or counselling if she or he has not done so well.

You can provide people with the opportunity to achieve, to exert influence and to grow by enlarging their jobs (giving them wider responsibilities), empowering them (giving them more responsibility), or by progressively extending the scope of the assignments you give them to provide additional challenges which will stretch and develop them.

Managing expectations

One of your key jobs as a line manager is to manage expectations. You have to ensure that your people know what they are expected to do and how they will be rewarded if they do it. This is in line with the motivation theories relating to expectations and goal setting which were described in Chapter 2.

You will be helped in doing this if the organisation has introduced a performance-management system as described in Chapter 9. But you do not have to wait for this (in some organisations you may have to wait a long time). Performance management is something any good manager does; it is not a personnel management technique.

In the light of what you know about managing people, motivation theory and what has been written earlier in this book, set out below as many things to do that you can think of which will motivate your staff, achieve higher levels of performance and enhance your reputation as someone who makes things happen.

A list of ten approaches is given in the Answers section on page 117.

What managers need to know and do about the reward system

Tick one only:

1. ☐ I do not really need to know very much. It is all managed by the personnel department and when it comes to fixing or reviewing salaries I just do what I am told.
2. ☐ To manage rewards effectively and to get the most out of the system I must know its ins and outs – not just the pay structure and policy guidelines but why it looks like it does and how it works.

If you tick (1) you are, it is to be hoped, one of a dwindling band of line managers who are the creatures of an autocratic organisation and a highly centralised and authoritarian personnel function. There are fewer and fewer organisations like this, but those that survive (although not for long) are remarkably successful at reducing their managers to ciphers and therefore destroying any real chance of getting real added value from rewards.

If you tick (2) you recognise that responsibility must

accompany empowerment and you cannot exert responsibility without understanding.

Knowledge of reward systems
On the basis of what you already know and what you have read in this book, list below the key things which you need to know about reward systems:

_____

_____

_____

A suggested list is given in the Answers section at the end of this chapter (pages 117–18).

Skills required to manage rewards
To manage your own reward system you will need skills as well as knowledge. What skills do you think you should possess?

_____

_____

_____

A suggested list is given in the Answers section (page 118).

Application of knowledge and skills

You can acquire all the knowledge about the system and develop all the skills you need to run it but you will still be confronted with issues where you have to exercise judgement in applying the knowledge and skills and in interpreting policy guidelines. You will have to exercise this judgement in the day-to-day contacts with your staff and the last thing you should want to do is to run to the personnel department for help.

The following are some typical situations.

1. You have 20 people working in your team. You know that 5 of them are really carrying the rest and you want to pay each of them the maximum PRP award of 10 per cent. The amount allowed for the increase to your payroll budget is 4 per cent, which means you could give a 3 per cent (the minimum) increase to 10 of your staff who are reliable if not exciting and pay nothing to the remaining 5 team members, all of whom you inherited when you took over the department and who, in your opinion, need to get the message that they are not up to scratch.

Your proposed distribution – 25 per cent getting the maximum, 50 per cent getting the minimum and 25 percent getting nothing – conflicts with the distribution guidelines issued by the personnel department. Your personnel manager, somewhat officiously (he's that sort of person), tells you to fall in line. What do you do?

2. One of the core members of your department who, while he has certain limitations, is a valued team member has hit the top of his salary scale. There is nowhere else for him to go and company policy is very firm that no one in a job should be paid more than the top rate for that job. What can you do about it and how do you explain it to him?

3. You have interviewed three short-listed external candidates for a key new job in your department. The job was advertised internally but no one remotely suitable applied and to your certain knowledge there is no one in your department qualified to do it. The job is, however, graded at the same level as the jobs held by your three team leaders.

There is one outstanding candidate. She has all the qualifications and knowhow you want and her experience in her present firm is highly relevant. She would like to join you because it will be a real opportunity for her to broaden her experience and use her skills even more effectively. Unfortunately, for you that is, her present firm also appreciates her work and are paying her above market rate. Your candidate is indeed very keen about your job and would accept a horizontal move (she is motivated more by the need to achieve than by money). However, even a horizontal move would mean that she would be paid way over the top of the scale for the grade – some 15 per cent more than any of your long-serving team leaders. You have enough money in your staff budget to take this person on at the rate she requests but not enough to increase the rate of pay of the other team leaders by 15 per cent immediately. How do you handle this situation?

4. You are conducting an annual performance review meeting which, as part of a performance-management system, sets out to achieve agreement between you and each member of your team on what the latter's objectives should be over the next period and on any plans for improving performance and developing competence.

The person you are interviewing has been in your department for five years. His job is processing customer queries and complaints. He has to acknowledge letters or answer telephone calls and answer, or find out the answer, to the query or deal with the complaint. He will do this by telephone or by letter. There are a number of standard letters, paragraphs or phrases for common queries or complaints which he can put together on his word processor. There has recently been an increased emphasis on improving levels of customer service and you are not happy that this individual is meeting acceptable standards for speed or response, turn-around of letters or, importantly, handling puzzled or angry customers over the telephone.

The company operates a performance-related pay scheme which is governed by the ratings managers give their staff on the basis of an analysis of achievement against objectives. The average PRP award is 3 per cent of pay and the next payment is due in nine months' time.

During the meeting the individual is clearly on the defensive. He knows you are not happy with his performance and he is ready to argue with any point you make. You are therefore careful to base your comments entirely on factual evidence: you have statistics on how many letters a day this individual processes compared with his colleagues (average 16 on his part compared with 22 on theirs – the target is 20). You also know on the basis of checks that his average turnaround is two days while on the whole the others turn around letters within the targeted time of 24 hours. Additionally, he receives a higher number of second letters expressing dissatisfaction with the initial reply (8 per cent of the total compared with the target of 4 per cent and the overall average of 3 per cent). You have overheard him on three occasions in the last month being impatient or even downright rude to a customer on the telephone.

His performance is clearly unsatisfactory but you want to give him the chance to improve. You therefore suggest that over the next six months he must meet the targets for processing and turnaround. You also make it clear that you will tolerate no more rudeness to customers.

He refuses to accept any of this. He says the targets are unreasonable, he is working as hard as he can, and if the others are doing better it is because they have easier letters to deal with (as the most experienced member of the team he claims that he is given the difficult ones – a claim which you know to be unfounded). What do you do?

5. A valued member of your staff comes to you with a letter offering her a job very similar to what she is doing now but at a substantially higher salary (20 per cent). She says she does not want to leave but it is difficult to turn down this increase – she needs the money. She asks if there is anything you can do.

For various reasons she is, in fact, paid about 10 per cent less than her (male) colleagues doing similar work. She is also someone to whom you intend to give an outstanding rating at the next pay review in three months' time. This should produce an 8 per cent increase on the basis of previous distributions. How do you deal with this?

Answers to these questions are suggested on pages 118–21.

Answers

Approaches to performance improvement (page 112)
Managing expectations involves motivating your staff. The following list suggests how this may be done.

1. Discuss and agree objectives which are SMART, ie stretching, measurable, attainable, relevant and time-related.
2. Get people to 'own' their objectives – if they agree that they can be achieved, even with some difficulty, then they are more likely to go for them.
3. Provide feedback immediately after the event – do not wait until the annual performance review.
4. Reinforce success – give credit where credit is due and praise where praise is deserved.
5. Take a positive and helpful view of failure: 'What can *we* do to ensure that it won't happen again?'
6. When holding a performance review meeting look forward not back. The purpose is to plan the future not dwell on the past.
7. Trust people to use their own methods to attain your ends.
8. Agree work and improvement plans on the basis of a positive will to trust and enable.
9. Appreciate that every work problem can be solved in such a way as to develop people's capacity to handle it.
10. See the task of managing people as a process of continuous improvement – of your own skills as a manager as well as theirs.

Knowledge of reward systems required (page 113)
Managers need to know:

- The reward strategies and policies of the organisation.
- How reliable information can be obtained on market rates.
- Details of the job evaluation scheme – how it operates and the part you have to play.

- The basis upon which jobs are graded.
- The rationale behind the pay structure.
- How the pay of employees progresses through the pay structure.
- The guidelines on fixing rates of pay on appointment or promotion.
- The guidelines on how to rate performance for performance-related pay purposes.
- The role you play in operating the company's performance management scheme.

Skills required to run the reward system (page 113)

These skills will be useful:

- Job analysis – understanding the demands made by jobs on job holders
- Job design – constructing jobs which provide job holders with the maximum amount of intrinsic motivation through achievement, responsibility and growth
- Use of motivation theory to understand the needs and motives of individuals and, therefore, how best to motivate them
- Rating – ability to make consistent, fair and defensible performance ratings
- Interpersonal skills in dealing with people, especially when reviewing performance or agreeing objectives.

Case studies (pages 114–16)

1. Take another hard look at your ratings. Are you sure you have got them right? Also think hard about the impact on those who will get no increase. How will you explain it to them? How will you use this negative action positively to obtain an improvement in performance? If they take this up through the grievance procedure will you be able to defend your actions successfully to higher authority?

If you are satisfied with the answers to all these questions stick to your guns. You are within your budget and you are doing what you believe, with good reason, to be the best thing for your department.

If the personnel manager continues to complain tell him, but not in so many words, to get lost, pointing out that it is you, not he, who is accountable for the performance of your department and you are doing what you believe to be right to improve that performance. The personnel manager might take this up with higher authority (your boss) so you will have to be prepared to justify your proposed action to him or her.

2. If company policies permit, you can recommend him for an attainment or sustained excellent performance bonus, but only if he fully deserves it. And the impression must not be given that this will become an annual entitlement – a gift that goes on giving. It has to be earned. Even if there is not a company policy for such bonuses you can press for such a payment as a special case, if it *is* a special case.

If it is not possible to pay a bonus in a deserving case, or if you do not believe that the case is deserving enough, then you simply have to explain as gently as possible that he has achieved the maximum rate for his job as laid down by company policy and that this rate, which is significantly higher than the average rate for the job, does recognise his experience and contribution.

3. If you are absolutely certain that this individual is vital to your department you may have to consider taking her on at her market rate. But before doing so you have got to weigh the balance between the advantages of obtaining her and the disadvantages of angering, demotivating or even losing the other members of your staff. If the balance of advantage is still in favour of engaging her then you may have to be prepared to explain why you took her on at this rate (market worth imperatives). You can explain to the aggrieved individuals that at the next salary review their pay will be considered in relation to their market worth as compared with external rates and adjustments will be made as appropriate and possible within budget constraints.

4. This is a fairly typical situation and dealing with it needs good interpersonal skills. Clearly, you cannot allow the present level of performance to continue. You have to do your best by reference to the facts of the situation (eg that the individual does *not* get the more difficult calls or letters) to convince him that there is room for improvement and that at least he should set his sights on the targets even if he does not achieve them straight away. You could offer further guidance, even training, on improving throughput, but such a suggestion might be rejected if the individual is convinced that he knows it all (as may well be the case with this person).

Ultimately, you have no choice but to insist that the targets are entirely reasonable and to express your conviction that he is quite capable of attaining them. You should tell him that you will review the situation with him again in, say, one month's time (not too long a period) to see what progress has been made. In no circumstances should you issue any threats of disciplinary action at this stage. Give him the chance to improve. But as a precaution against a possible future unfair dismissal case, make a note for your file on the discussion.

Incidentally, this is a situation where a PRP scheme with a possible payout of 3 per cent in nine months' time is not going to have any effect on performance at all.

5. The reactions in such a case would be either to refuse to submit to this 'blackmail' or at the other extreme, to offer her a 20 per cent increase. Neither of these reactions is appropriate. Employees have often tried to 'blackmail' their employers in such situations and it is best to resist blatant attempts to do so. But this is not a blatant attempt. However, to pay the full amount could well be excessive. Although there may be rare occasions when such an action is justifiable because an individual *is* invaluable or because he or she is clearly underpaid, this is not entirely the situation in this case. What you could do, if your budget allowed it, is to recommend an immediate increase of 10 per cent to bring her into line with her colleagues (which should happen anyway) and indicate, without committing yourself, that if she continues to perform as well as she has done she should be given a sufficiently high award at the next pay review in three months' time to make up most, if not all, of the difference between what she will be paid and what she has been offered.

Further Information

Sources of market rate data

Monks Partnership, Debden Green, Saffron Walden, Essex CB11 3LX; Tel: 01799 542222.

Remuneration Economics Ltd, Surrey House, 51 Portland Road, Kingston-upon-Thames, Surrey KT1 2SH; Tel: 0181 549 8726.

Reward Group, Reward House, Stone Business Park, Staffordshire ST15 0SD.

Incomes Data Services – Management Pay Review, 193 St John Street, London EC1V 4LS; Tel 0171 250 3434.

Industrial Relations Services – Pay and Benefits Bulletin, 18–20 Highbury Place, London N5 1QP; Tel 0171 354 5858.

Further reading

Armstrong, M and Murlis, H. *Reward Management* (3rd edition). Kogan Page (1994)

Pritchard, D and Murlis, H. *Jobs, Roles and People: The New World of Job Evaluation*. Nicholas Brearley (1992)

Armstrong, M. *Performance Management*. Kogan Page (1994)

Cannell, M and Wood, S. *Incentive Pay: Impact and Evolution*. Institute of Personnel and Development (1992)